Praise for *The Book of Awesome ...*

"Karen is an exceptional writer. She makes history digestible and easy to understand in an entertaining way. Her works are also inspiring and empowering! I loved learning about the strength and autonomy of so many unknown yet powerful Asian women (who, many times, were surpassing their male counterparts)! From warrior queens to brainy scientists to influential leaders, *The Book of Awesome Asian Women* brings stories too long omitted from mainstream narratives back to life, giving us life in the process!"

—Jacki Jing, actor, producer, and Netflix TV personality

"The powerful impact of Asian women on society is often overlooked. Karen Wang Diggs's new book remedies this. In *The Book of Awesome Asian Women*, Diggs highlights the lives and achievements of extraordinary Asian women from the past and present. Each chapter features inspiring stories, highlighting their significant contributions in various fields while addressing the unique challenges they faced due to their gender and cultural backgrounds. The writing is engaging and approachable, making it a compelling read for anyone interested in the unique journeys of these women. Readers will find it refreshing and inspiring."

—Nita Sweeney, author of *Depression Hates a Moving Target*

"If you love history and are keenly interested in celebrating outstanding women, this book is for you! In *The Book of Awesome Asian Women*, Karen Wang Diggs details the stories, struggles, and successes of extraordinary Asian women from various eras and all walks of life. Readers are introduced to more than 100 remarkable women across diverse fields—writers, scientists, athletes, activists, and even royalty.

What makes this book especially notable is its attention to detail; it provides rich insights into each of these incredible lives. *The Book of Awesome Asian Women* is not only a beautiful tribute book, but also a celebration of resilience, justice, empowerment, passion, and purpose. I'm inspired!"

—Sherry Richert Belul, founder of Simply Celebrate and author of *Say It Now* and *The Love List of a Lifetime*

A Celebration of Unsung Heroes:

"*The Book of Awesome Asian Women* sheds light on the untold narratives of trailblazing women who shaped history against all odds. Karen Wang Diggs captivates readers with vivid storytelling and compelling historical insights, proving that these stories deserve to be heard by generations to come. This book is both a revelation and a celebration!"

—MJ Fievre, author of *The Book of Awesome Black Women*

"Pop culture has long tried to put Asian women in pigeonholes, in varieties ranging from the docile 'Lotus Flower' to the hypersexualized 'Dragon Lady' to the materialistic 'Crazy Rich Asian.' Karen Wang Diggs's timely book dismantles gender and racial stereotypes by showcasing the amazing accomplishments of females from many Asian countries. It is a brilliant testament to their priceless contributions to the world."

—Marlene Wagman-Geller, author of *Unabashed Women: The Fascinating Biographies of Bad Girls, Seductresses, Rebels and One-of-a-Kind Women*

"In *The Book of Awesome Asian Women*, Karen Wang Diggs puts the spotlight on the phenomenal trailblazing Asian women throughout history who have courageously fought to clear the paths for future generations to thrive. This superbly written book connects us to a worldwide sisterhood of female ancestors, inspiring the quest to continue this empowered legacy. The chapters illuminate these mavericks' unwavering quest for equality, opportunity, and excellence in everything from science, the arts, and medicine to freedom fighting. These stories will embolden readers to embrace the limitless possibilities in their own lives—awakening the warrior within us all."

—Angela LoMenzo, author of *Wisdom of Wildly Creative Women*

THE BOOK OF
Awesome Asian Women

THE BOOK OF

Awesome Asian Women

Empresses, Warriors, Scientists, and Mavericks

Karen Wang Diggs

MIAMI

For permission requests, please contact the publisher at:

Mango Publishing Group

5966 South Dixie Highway, Suite 300

Miami, FL 33143

info@mango.bz

For special orders, quantity sales, course adoptions and corporate sales, please email the publisher at sales@mango.bz. For trade and wholesale sales, please contact Ingram Publisher Services at customer.service@ingramcontent.com or +1.800.509.4887.

The Book of Awesome Asian Women: Empresses, Warriors, Scientists, and Mavericks

Library of Congress Cataloging-in-Publication Number: 2024947455

ISBN: (print) 978-1-68481-723-8, (ebook) 978-1-68481-724-5

BISAC: BIO002020 BIOGRAPHY & AUTOBIOGRAPHY / Asian & Asian American

Printed in the United States of America

This book is dedicated to the two most awesome Asian women in my life:

my mother, Lisan Chang (張麗珊), and my aunt,

Chat-mei Yang (楊潔梅), who was from the last generation

of Chinese women to suffer from foot-binding.

Table of Contents

Foreword

As a famous Chinese proverb tells us, "Women hold up half the sky," but this book proves women hold up more than their half of the sky, and have in fact been doing amazing, remarkable, historic, and awesome things since the dawn of time. Karen Wang Diggs's *The Book of Awesome Asian Women* is long awaited, and as a herstorian, I for one have been longing for an awesome Asian woman to take up her pen and share these important stories with the world, including many that have remained untold until now. This is a book I will keep near at hand to reread and refer to. It is my sincere hope for every library, school, and bookstore to have copies of this vital work, and that it is available to as many people as possible. I feel it is especially important that it is available to students of all ages, especially children, and that teachers will take up this text to educate future generations about the achievements of Asian women from all over the world throughout history. This is a book I wish I'd had as a girl so I could soak up the stories of these glorious women.

From astronauts to astronomers, athletes, and academics, as well as queens, emperors, and warriors, the courage, strength, and brilliance of these women will hold you spellbound. The tale of how Wu Zetian went from her start as a concubine to ruling all of China is mesmerizing. You will be riveted by how the shaman Queen Himiko rose to become known as "Daughter of the Sun." The athletic achievements of many of these women induce feelings of hope and motivation, from Olympic skaters who battled the odds to groundbreaking skier Eileen Gu. Annette Lu went from jailed dissident to vice president of Taiwan. Mazlan binti Othman is an astrophysicist with the heart of a poet. Some of these amazing women you may know well from the silver screen, like beloved *Grey's Anatomy* actress Sandra Oh, or you may recognize them from their *New York Times* bestselling books, such as author Amy Tan, or from being a pop culture phenomenon like singer and performance artist Yoko Ono.

May this book inspire you to not let anything get in your way. These women are indomitable and strong-willed, and their belief in themselves compelled them to do and be their best, as we all should. My wish for you, dear reader, is that you uncover and celebrate your own personal awesomeness.

—Becca Anderson, bestselling author of *Badass Affirmations* and *The Book of Awesome Women*

Introduction

In the past few years, there has been a heightened awareness of the need to illuminate the priceless contributions that women and girls have made to humanity. It is encouraging that women are finally celebrated in all forms of visual arts, books, and music. However, the current shift toward parity of acknowledgement between the accomplishments of females and males is not entirely complete. Women of color, including Asian women, are still underrepresented or misrepresented.

As a Chinese American woman who has had to contend with the dual obstacle of racism and sexism, the process of attaining confidence and feeling secure has not been easy. When I was younger, even though I wasn't fully aware of the prejudices permeating the culture all around me, I felt an inward sense of not quite belonging and not being whole. Subconsciously, I was searching for a lost piece of myself. That search was rather frustrating because I had no idea what I was searching for, yet I knew I had to find it.

Eventually, I realized that the elusive object of my quest was right in front of me. I just needed to awaken to the reality that centuries of patriarchy, racism derived from colonialization, religious institutional structures, and culturally driven subjugation of women and girls have all converged into our present time with the effect of disorienting and diminishing me, along with countless other women, whether they are fully aware of the implications or not.

The Influence of Confucianism upon Asian Women

You may have the impression that Confucianism is a good and noble doctrine. After all, it is an ancient system created by a scholar named Kunfuzi, also known as Confucius, over 2,000 years ago, and one that is still revered by many people today. Confucianism has many noble points, such as filial piety, emphasis on education, cultivating the self to best benefit society, and other codes of conduct based on "Li" (proper cultural behavior) and "Ren" (the quality of being humane or compassionate).

However, there is a dark side to Confucianism, which has less to do with Confucius's original intent and more to do with the men who co-opted his doctrines to serve their own desires. A clear distinction should be made between the philosophy of Confucianism and its *politicization* throughout the centuries.

As Confucius himself did not compose any official texts, and because his students were still adding to *The Analects* centuries after he was long gone, no one is certain which ideas came directly from the Sage himself.

It wasn't until the Han Dynasty (206 BCE to 220 CE), several centuries after his death, that Confucianism became the official system of social behavior and statecraft, forming the foundation that defined Chinese culture for the next two millennia.

Overall, the Confucian classics barely addressed women, clearly demonstrating how little they mattered in the scheme of Confucianism. It was taken on face value that women should be subservient to men and that failure to observe the proper etiquette between the superior male and the inferior female, such as between a husband and wife or brother and sister, would cause social disharmony and a violation of the strict rules of conduct dictated in *The Analects*.

Over time, Confucianism spread into many countries in Asia. As a result, it harmed not only Chinese women but also women from other countries, such as Vietnam, Japan, Korea, and beyond. A repeated pattern of the decline of gender equality and systematic erosion of female power can be seen in historical events as politicians manipulated Confucianism to enforce their rule on society through restrictions on girls and women.

The primary issue that concerns us is that *The Analects* discriminated against women by isolating them from politics, education, and culture, in essence barring them from full participation in society.

Unfortunately, patriarchy was not only prevalent in Asia. On the other side of the world, other scholars and influential thinkers held ideas similar to those of Confucius and his disciples. One such was Aristotle (384–322 BCE), who lived a few centuries before Confucius. He clearly stated that women were physically weaker and morally and intellectually inferior to men and should be confined to the domestic sphere.

In Athenian society, women had specific purposes through which they were expected to support their homeland. A woman had to guard the house and perform specific duties for its proper functioning. And she had to give birth to many children—ideally male—to strengthen the family. Marriages primarily served social and religious purposes. Girls were married at a very young age to men whom their fathers chose. Women spent most of the day at their house, usually on the upper floor, knitting or weaving on the loom. These were the only activities that were considered suitable for elite women.

Thus, due to the heavy influence of male-centric philosophers such as Aristotle and Confucius, women in many countries became second-class citizens and have continued to struggle for their rights throughout the centuries.

Voices of Asian Women

From the perfectly attired geisha moving in her dainty choreographed gait to the fatal "dragon lady" darting out flames while drawing blood with her fang-like crimson nails, antiquated and racial stereotypes have significantly harmed and silenced the social and political achievements of Asian women around the world.

Western media has long portrayed Asian women in limited and cartoonish roles due to the suppressive forces that boxed Asian women in for centuries. Stereotypes like the submissive geisha or the hyper-manipulative "dragon lady" have reinforced these narrow views. In addition, many Asian cultures have traditional gender roles that emphasize women as caretakers and supporters, further reinforcing such stereotypes.

If we listen carefully, we can hear the voices of brilliant females, past and present, beckoning us to be brave and stand up for sovereignty over our destinies. For despite the suffocating weight of patriarchy, women have played pivotal roles in shaping the political, economic, scientific, and cultural landscapes of societies. Their voices also encourage us to be open-hearted daughters, sisters, wives, mothers, lovers, teachers, and leaders.

Now, let us turn the page and be dazzled by stories of awesome Asian women who are symbols of resilience, hope, and female sovereignty.

It is my sincere wish that *The Book of Awesome Asian Women* will shine bright as a beacon to unite and strengthen the bond of sisterhood between women of all nationalities—a beacon of the hope that all people will come to recognize our shared humanity.

CHAPTER ONE

SHE DARED TO RULE—QUEENS, EMPRESSES, AND HEADS OF STATE

Half of the world's population is female, yet men still hold the majority
of political power, leaving women underrepresented. For a fairer, more
sustainable, and more peaceful world, it's essential to have gender
equality in leadership—especially now, as we face climate challenges
and endless wars. Research shows that women often bring strong
communication skills, helping bridge political divides and nurturing
cooperation. With more women in government, issues like child care,
health care, and the environment tend to get the attention they deserve.

Throughout history, there have been few female rulers, and those who
stepped up to lead were often judged harshly because of ingrained
patriarchy. But women have always shown incredible strength,
intelligence, and resilience. In this chapter, you'll meet queens,

empresses, and heads of state—past and present—who made a lasting impact despite facing tremendous obstacles. They light the way forward for a future of female empowerment.

Wu Zetian—from Concubine to Empress

During the course of her life, this remarkable woman was a concubine, a nun, a seductress, a mother, a poet, and the Empress of China. Empress Wu, named Wu Zhao at birth, was born into a high-ranking family during the beginning of the Tang Dynasty. Her family claimed their ancestral lineage descended from the founder of Daoism, Lao Tzu. She was well-educated in history, literature, music, poetry, and calligraphy. Due to her father's close ties with the imperial court, she entered the privileged retinue of Emperor Taizong's court as his concubine at the age of thirteen.

Side note on concubinage in China:

For hundreds of years, it was common practice for men, especially those of the ruling class, to have concubines in their households in addition to so-called "official wives." Men were not allowed to have more than two official wives, but they could have as many concubines as they could afford.

Girls between the ages of thirteen to sixteen were routinely selected by scouts and presented to these male elites. If selected, they essentially entered into a life of slavery in service of their masters.

The communist Chinese government finally abolished this misogynistic practice in 1957. However, it wasn't deemed illegal in Hong Kong until 1978.

Despite her youth, Wu exhibited clear signs of exceptional intelligence and the ability to align herself with political power. Through a combination of innate acumen, a high-spirited character, and physical beauty, she quickly became the emperor's favorite. He made her his private secretary so that she could travel with him. She was also given access to governmental documents. This very privileged exposure to affairs of state honed the future empress's political prowess.

She noticed that the emperor's son, Li Zhi, who was next in line for the throne, had a big crush on her. Since he was much closer to her in age than his father, she was fully aware of the potential of his infatuation and used her charms and good looks to keep him under her spell. This tactic would serve her well after the emperor died in 645 CE. Upon his death, Emperor Taizong's entire harem was sent to a monastery. The custom was that these unfortunate women were then supposed to pray for their dearly departed lord for the rest of their days, meaning that the women had to give up their finery, shave off their hair, and don the drab grey robes of the nunnery. This, however, did not impede Wu's ability to climb up the "imperial ladder."

Li Zhi ascended the imperial throne after his father's death and became Emperor Gaozong. He often visited the monastery where Wu Zhao was confined. His excuse was that he was in mourning for his father and wanted to pray for him there, but in reality, the new emperor was using that as a pretext to meet with his object of desire. Even with a bald head and lackluster attire, Wu Zhao was able to seduce him. Despite his ministers advising caution, he brought her back to court as his high-ranking concubine. This would prove to be the start of how Wu Zhao was able to bend him to her will.

In the next few years, Wu Zhao gave birth to five children, four of whom were males. She was now the mother of royal sons, and this made her unstoppable. At this juncture, the rumors of Wu Zhao's ruthless tactics to gain absolute power become rather bloody in nature. It is said that she "removed" Gaozong's official first wife by accusing her of murdering a child and was also successful at ousting his other favorite concubines and their children. Now that Wu Zhao was fully ensconced in a commanding position, even the emperor was afraid of her because he belatedly realized at this point that she was far more cunning and manipulative than he could ever imagine. He consented to let her assist him in managing state affairs, and she quickly established a system of informants and used it to root out any opposition to her authority.

In the year 660, at the relatively young age of thirty-two, Emperor Gaozong suffered a stroke that blinded him. As a result of his infirmity, he assigned all state affairs to Empress Wu, making her the unofficial ruler of the empire until he died in 683 CE. Some suspected she fed him just enough poison to subdue but not kill him.

Under the law, Empress Wu could not herself become the emperor because there was a rule against women from becoming the Emperor of China; however, that didn't stop Wu. Remember her sons? Initially, she placed two of her sons in succession on the throne, but they were both just puppets under the tight strings of her control. Eventually, Wu chose to disregard conventions and declared herself "Holy and Divine Emperor" in 690.

Although Empress Wu may seem like a murderous femme fatale, it is important to note that history in China, which was written by men and steeped in patriarchal attitudes, greatly distorted Wu's reign, casting her as a power-hungry villain and overlooking her many positive contributions.

Here are six significant advancements that Empress Wu accomplished
during her reign:

1. Civil Service Reform:
    She reformed the civil service system by mandating equal access
    to high-ranking government jobs. This made it possible for
    anyone (only men in those days) to advance in the governmental
    hierarchy based solely on his diligence and intellect rather than on
    family connections.

2. Expansion of Territory:
    Under her military strategy, the Tang Dynasty greatly expanded
    its territory and sphere of influence.

3. Improved Farming Practices:
    Empress Wu had a keen interest in agriculture. Under her reign,
    she set up major irrigation projects and even lifted the farm tax
    for several years so that farmers became prosperous and there was
    always sufficient food.

4. Spread of Buddhism and Tolerance of Other Religions:
    Other religions were supported in addition to Buddhism because
    Empress Wu was very accepting in her attitudes and allowed
    people in her realm to worship as they pleased.

5. Patron of the Arts:
    Empress Wu also made the theater and other artistic
    performances free to attend, giving the populace a heightened
    appreciation for art and poetry. During her reign, creative
    entertainments were not only for the rich to enjoy. Some events in
    that era had over 700 performers!

6. Women's Rights:
    Empress Wu started a series of campaigns to elevate women's
    rights in Chinese society and encouraged the writing of
    biographies of exemplary women. She herself wrote a volume
    entitled *Biographies of Famous Women* to emphasize her point.

Another bold change she made was to require children to mourn each of their parents when they died, rather than only their father, as had been the traditional practice.

Under her influence, women had some latitude and freedom regarding remarriage, sex, and equitable participation in society. After her death, the Tang Dynasty experienced its Golden Age, mainly because the general populace had ready access to education and appreciation for the arts. Many modern scholars, now freed from the restraints of Confucianism, which denied women an equal place in society, have credited Empress Wu for her many political accomplishments and her role in paving the way for future female rulers.

Queen Himiko—Daughter of the Sun

One ancient shero, Queen Himiko, was featured in *Tomb Raider* (both the 2013 video game and the 2018 movie). This is rather extraordinary given that this woman, who is recognized as a shaman queen, lived over 1,800 years ago and was deliberately left out of historical records for a few hundred years. Yet now, in the twenty-first century, she has become one of the most iconic female rulers from Japan's ancient past.

Some people still question Queen Himiko's existence. However, sufficient historical records and archaeological evidence exist to prove that this mythical queen was not a myth but a real person who reigned over her people and her kingdom in the third century.

To be clear, the version of Queen Himiko featured in *Tomb Raider* was *not* based on facts. All the details, save her name and country of origin, were massively embellished for the sole purpose of Hollywood-style entertainment.

Himiko started her reign in 190 CE and would remain at the helm for almost fifty years. The territory of Queen Himiko's tribe comprised approximately thirty clans that joined together to form a confederation known as Yamatai.

In ancient Japanese, *Himiko* means "Sun Child" or "Daughter of the Sun." This name refers to her divine origin as a direct descendant of Amaterasu, the most revered deity of the Shinto religion. Amaterasu is known as the divinity who illuminates heaven. All subsequent rulers of Japan claimed to be descended from Amaterasu.

The Japanese did not have a written language until the sixth century, so historians have relied upon chronicles from China and Korea to substantiate the reign of Queen Himiko, along with archaeological evidence that has come to light in recent centuries.

China and the highly patriarchal doctrines of Confucianism had a significant influence on Japan. Since the acknowledgement and inclusion of female shaman rulers did not fit into the male-centric worldview dictated by the men in power during those centuries, Queen Himiko and other rulers of her sex were snubbed.

The Yamatai Kingdom fared quite well under Queen Himiko's rule. In addition to upholding her religious, shamanistic, and political duties, Himiko presided over more than 100 states that acknowledged her sovereignty within the Country of Wa. According to records, there were more than seventy thousand households in her realm, as well as thriving trade and agriculture, well-organized laws, and a taxation system. Her subjects enjoyed general peace and prosperity.

Himiko died in 248 CE, and records state that she was interred in a grand keyhole-shaped *kofun*, or tomb, measuring 100 paces in diameter, equivalent to about 150 meters or almost 500 feet. Now, that is a huge burial site. And from Chinese records, we know that over 100 male and female attendants followed her to her mausoleum.

Like a supernatural being who can come back from the grave, Queen Himiko has come back to life—well, at least in Japan's historical records and pop culture. She now holds the distinction of being Japan's first named and recognized ruler. Even more striking is that according to a recent Ministry of Education and Sciences survey, 99 percent of Japanese schoolchildren know of her and her role in history.

After Himiko's death, a man came to sit on the throne. However, he was very unpopular, and an uprising ensued. Another woman was elected; her name was Iyo. Although she was a girl of just thirteen, she managed to reinstate peace by following the same political ethos that Himiko had established. Iyo was none other than Queen Himiko's niece, another real-life female shaman sovereign, and like Himiko was believed to be descended from the goddess Amaterasu.

Razia Sultan—the People's Queen

Razia Sultan's short but brilliant reign of three and a half years was a spectacular display of courage, astute military strategies, judicious administrative decisions, and radical policies that benefited her subjects regardless of race or religion. Her brilliance, however, burned out all too soon due to jealousy, betrayal, and the odious and patriarchal closed-minded attitudes of highly conservative men who were only concerned with their hold on privilege, power, and monetary gains.

The term "sultan" refers to a sovereign, particularly one who is Muslim and male. In the history of Islam, there have only been a few female sultans. Razia Sultan (Raziyyat-Ud-Dunya Wa Ud-Din) ascended the throne at age thirty-one.

Razia's father was Shams ud Din Iltutmish, a greatly respected sultan who ruled northern India from Delhi. Just before his death, he shocked his advisors by appointing his daughter as the next sultan.

When asked by his astonished advisors why he would do such a thing, the sultan replied: "My sons are given over to the follies of youth: none of them is fit to be king and rule this country, and you will find no one better able to do so than my daughter."

Before Razia could become the sultan, she had to face an aristocratic all-male advisory team known as the Forty Emirs, who were not about to let a female rule above them. They outvoted her and instead placed Firuz Shah, the son of Razia's power-grabbing stepmother, on the throne. Rather than protesting, Razia bided her time.

Sure enough, Firuz was utterly inept and corrupt. Within a year of his reign, the citizenry rebelled, and the usurper was forced out and jailed.

The Forty Emirs, shamed by their support of Firuz Shah and his mother, had no choice but to honor Sultan Iltutmish's edict. Razia Sultan was finally crowned on November 19, 1236, fulfilling her father's dying wish. The Forty Emirs, however, were not about to relinquish their prejudice against having a female sultan. To them, Razia was an insult to their male-dominated regime, so as soon as she ascended the throne, they started plotting against her.

Although Razia Sultan's reign was brief, she accomplished a great deal, initiating reforms such as lower taxes and including Hindus in her court, as well as expanding territories and keeping the Mongols away just as her father had while sustaining peace and prosperity in the land. She was a patron of the arts who supported education and was commonly known as "The People's Queen." She did all this while constantly battling the Emirs, who were always looking for faults to point out in efforts to unseat her.

She also was not afraid to remove her veil and, on several occasions, she even rode an elephant into battle!

As you can imagine, all this was too much for the Forty Emirs, who took every opportunity to disrupt Razia's rising power, popularity, and reputation as an able sovereign.

When Razia left the capital on a campaign to quell some unrest in a nearby province, the Emirs put their treacherous plans into motion. First, they assassinated her trusted advisor, and then they waged a war of insurrection against Razia herself. In the ensuing battle, she was taken prisoner. As fate would have it, the person in charge of her captivity was a childhood friend named Altunia. While Razia was locked up in Altunia's castle, she rekindled his affection for her. They married, and Altunia switched sides and declared war against the Emirs. On October 13, 1240, the enemies met; but sadly, the outcome did not favor the queen or her new spouse, and they were both killed. Razia had ruled for three years, six months, and six days.

A statement by the well-known historian Juzjani illustrates the poignant truth as he memorializes Razia Sultan with these words:

A great monarch, wise, just, generous, a benefactor to her realm, a dispenser of equity, the protector of her people, and leader of her armies... She had all kingly qualities, except her sex, and this exception made all her virtues of no effect in the eyes of men.

Razia Sultan is considered a folk hero in India today and is widely
admired. The rise and fall of her reign continue to fascinate and inspire.

Khatun Sorghaghtani Beki—from War Bride to Maker of Khans

Mongolia is a land of endless sky and steppes that stretch to eternity. It is
a magnificent yet extremely harsh country that has produced one of the
fiercest conquerors in history.

Genghis Khan rose from extremely impoverished circumstances
to become the supreme Khan. He united all the disparate tribes of
Mongolia into an unstoppable fighting force. His empire bordered on
modern-day Russia and Europe, and included China, India, Persia, and
the Middle East. Thanks to modern DNA technology, it is now known
that some sixteen million people alive are direct descendants of this
formidable ruler.

It is unfortunate that today, the Mongolian Empire is associated with an
inherently male-dominated image. In reality, Mongolian women have
always played an integral part in Mongol society. In addition to caring
for their children, domestic affairs, and herd animals, women were
also warriors. Under Genghis Khan's rule, every man *and* woman was
trained to keep the nation ready for battle. Mongolian women knew how
to use a bow and arrow, were expert horsewomen, and even participated
in wrestling contests. Genghis Khan considered his daughters more
capable of governing his vast empire than his sons. One of his daughters-
in-law, Sorghaghtani Beki, proved herself genuinely worthy of the title
of *khatun* (queen). She was a brilliant female leader, wife, and mother, a
politician extraordinaire, and a ruthless, vengeful enemy when necessary

to secure power for herself and her four sons. Thus, she ensured that Genghis Khan's direct bloodline continued to rule the khanate.

Sorghaghtani Beki was from a noble family of the Kerayit tribe, which Genghis Khan subjugated in 1203. Sorghaghtani was given as a war bride to Tolui, one of Genghis Khan's sons. Fortunately for the young Kerayit princess, her betrothed was a very good man and an able warrior. The young royal couple had four sons. By many accounts, Tolui greatly respected and depended upon his wife and consulted with her on all matters relating to governing the empire, including military campaigns.

Unfortunately, Tolui died on a campaign in 1233 when he was only forty, leaving his wife to both raise their four sons alone and govern the territories he had inherited from his father, Genghis Khan. She stubbornly and strategically refused marriage proposals from powerful men after her husband's death and devoted her time and energy to grooming her four sons to rule after her, as well as to governing the lands that she inherited as Tolui's widow. Although Sorghaghtani was illiterate, she was gifted with exceptional innate intelligence. She was a capable leader with extraordinary diplomatic skills and a nurturing and wise mother who made sure that her sons received the best possible training for becoming future Khans of the Mongolian Empire.

Sorghaghtani was a Nestorian Christian, yet she taught her sons to be tolerant of all religions. It was recorded that she promoted Islamic laws and gave large donations to the poor, places of worship, and schools until her death. She had the wisdom and keen psychological foresight to understand that in order to rule other peoples and maintain that rule, the Mongols had to adapt and gain the favor and trust of local populations. Instead of war and pillage, she ensured the peasants were never exploited and actively promoted local economies and trade.

After Genghis Khan's death, there were different rulers for over a decade, and things were very unsettled. Eventually, discord among the many Mongolian tribes began to endanger their power and the territories they had conquered during Genghis Khan's rule.

At this pivotal juncture, Khatun Sorghaghtani called for a *kurultai* to settle the matter. During this assembly, all the groundwork she had laid in the past bore fruit. Members of the tribal council unanimously voted in her eldest son, Mongke, to be the next Great Khan.

Although she died in 1261, soon after Mongke Khan became the Khan of all Mongolia and the Mongols' conquered territories, Khatun Sorghaghtani Beki's influence continued through the legacy of her four sons. In addition to Mongke, her second son, Kublai Khan, founded the Yuan Dynasty in China, which lasted almost a century, and another son, Hulagu, became Khan of Persia and Georgia.

Before her death, Sorghaghtani Beki handpicked all of the senior wives for each of her sons. These daughters-in-law went on to have measurable positive influences on her sons and on the governance of their respective domains.

Without her courage, intelligence, wisdom, vision, and maternal care, Genghis Khan might not have had his direct descendants carry on his vast empire, and Kublai Khan, his grandson, may never have become the monarch who ruled over China and parts of the Mongol Empire.

One Persian historian described Khatun Sorghaghtani Beki as "extremely intelligent and able" and "towering above all the women in the world."

Queen Seondeok—Astronomer, Sovereign, Shaman, and Seer

Not much is known about Queen Seondeok's early life. She was born around 606 CE and was named Princess Deokman at birth. She was the oldest of three girls born from the union of King Jinpyoeng and Queen Ma-Ya. Because Queen Ma-Ya did not give birth to a boy, she was sent away, and King Jinpyoeng took another wife. Ironically, as fate would have it, his second wife also failed to bear a son.

He was going to pass his seat to his son-in-law, Yongchun, but Seondeok was a very persuasive strategist, and she convinced her father that *she* was the right and most competent heir to the throne. She was brilliant in astronomy and mathematics; thus, brainpower was the outstanding feature that lifted this brilliant young woman up to take the reins of power. Princess Deokman, who was then crowned Queen Seondeok, became the twenty-seventh ruler of Silla in 632 CE and the first female monarch in Korean history.

Another remarkable thing about this young lady was that she was a shaman, in tune with the mysterious forces of nature while also embracing the humanistic and compassionate aspects of Zen Buddhism and Daoism. She became famous for her gift of clairvoyance, which she used successfully to repel a large army from the hostile state of Paekche. This famous incident occurred five years into her reign. In the winter of 627 CE, hundreds of frogs descended into a pond near her royal residence where they croaked continually all day and all night, which was highly unusual. After considering all the signs and omens, Queen Seondeok ordered two of her best generals to take a contingent of 2,000 men and ride west to a valley known as the Cradle of Life. When her generals and troops arrived, they found an encampment of over 500 Paekche soldiers lying in wait to launch a surprise attack on Silla. The queen's army quickly defeated not only the concealed force of 500 but also 1,200 more Paekche soldiers who were sent as reinforcements.

Let's look at the many impressive accomplishments Queen Seondeok achieved during her sixteen-year reign. Her domestic policies were very successful, and Silla enjoyed a flourishing of literature and other arts, as well as the sciences. She emphasized providing equal educational opportunity for both sexes, and she did a lot as a ruler to benefit the common people, and by so doing ushered in a period of prosperity. It is recorded that shortly after her coronation, she gained the trust and loyalty of her subjects by sending royal inspectors to every province to oversee the care and welfare of widows, widowers, orphans, and the poor and elderly who had no families to support them. This benevolent and strategic move weakened any opposition to her rule by the male aristocracy.

She was also a patron of Buddhism, and many fine temples were built during her reign. She had her architects design a beautiful nine-tiered pagoda that also functioned as a strategic watch tower to prevent unforeseen attacks on Silla. This was the largest Korean pagoda ever built, and at its completion, it held the record as the tallest structure in East Asia and the world! It was 263 feet (eighty meters) tall. This pagoda stood for centuries until the fierce warriors of Genghis Khan burned it down in 1238.

The most magnificent structure that Queen Seondeok commissioned was a stargazing observatory that is still standing today. It is located 200 miles from Seoul and stands twenty-eight feet high. It is constructed from precisely 365 stones, one for each day of the year. There are twelve base stones positioned in a square, three on each side, representing the four seasons and the twelve months of the year. It is known as

Cheomseongdae ("the Tower of the Moon and Stars"). It is the oldest astronomical tower anywhere in the world.

Seondeok was also a skillful matchmaker who encouraged matrimonial alliances that would benefit the future of not only Silla but all of Korea. The marriages she arranged between several prominent families created a power bloc that would later enable Silla to unify the Korean Peninsula and end the fragmentation of the Three Kingdoms.

She also successfully quelled an attempted revolt by a once-trusted courtier. Shortly after that, she correctly predicted her own death to the exact date. One day, she assembled her court and announced, "I will surely die on February 17, 647." Her courtiers were puzzled as she was in perfect health. To everyone's amazement, Queen Seondeok died due to an unspecified illness on the exact date she predicted. Although she had a male consort during her reign, she was childless. She was much respected and beloved by her people, and under her leadership, the Silla Kingdom entered its Golden Age. Two more female rulers would follow her on the throne after her death.

Queen Indradevi and Queen Jayarajadevi— Monarchs of a Golden Age

Modern Cambodia is a small heart-shaped country, approximately the size of the US state of Washington; it is set between Laos, Vietnam, and the Gulf of Thailand. During the ninth to thirteenth centuries, Cambodia, which was then much larger, was known as the Khmer Empire (sometimes called the Angkorian Empire). France colonized Cambodia in the 1800s. It gained independence in 1954, but a year later, the country had to deal with the detrimental effects of the Vietnam War, which also embroiled Cambodia. Today, Cambodia functions under a constitutional monarchy, and its people are struggling to gain complete independence.

Let us now travel back to Cambodia's Golden Age during the twelfth century and learn how two women played an instrumental role in the flourishing of a great civilization. The capital then was Angkor Thom, with over one million inhabitants. It was a magnificent metropolis with well-constructed canals and dams, a thriving urban center, an agricultural system that produced a surplus for trade, and numerous temples that supported its inhabitants' religious and spiritual evolution. Keep in mind that Europe at this time was just beginning to awaken out of the Dark Ages, and people there were dying from famine and plagues. Women in particular had very few rights in feudal Europe, not to mention education.

King Jayavarman VII ascended to the throne of the Khmer Empire in 1181 and ruled Cambodia for almost forty years. He expanded the Cambodian Kingdom to its furthest geographical extent, which included parts of modern-day Vietnam, Laos, and Thailand. What is less known is that he married two sisters—forgotten heroines who brought about social progress and improvements in women's rights while they were wives to King Jayavarman VII, to whom history has given much of the credit.

These two sisters were named Jayarajadevi and Indradevi. They profoundly influenced their royal husband and guided him to transform the Khmer Empire into a country where both men and women were respected and citizens enjoyed universal education and health care. Unfortunately, very little is known about Jayarajadevi and Indradevi's personal lives.

King Jayavarman VII, Queen Jayarajadevi, and Queen Indradevi are often referred to as "the Royal Trinity," because together, they transformed the lives of their people. To be clear, Jayavarman was not married to both sisters at the same time. Jayarajadevi, the younger sister, was his first wife. Historical records state that before he was crowned king, she waited and worried when a political rival forced him into temporary exile during the early years of their marriage. Eventually, he was able to return to the capital and subsequently attained the throne.

After they were established as the king and queen of the empire, Jayarajadevi gave up her entire inheritance, which must have been substantial as she was from a royal family. She did that because she was genuinely concerned about the welfare of others and placed her spiritual growth ahead of mundane worldly matters. It is speculated that this young queen was strongly influenced by her older sister, Indradevi, a Buddhist teacher and scholar.

It is known that Jayarajadevi started building several schools dedicated to educating orphans and young women. Sadly, she died just a few years after her husband became the monarch. The King then married her sister Indradevi. Under her guidance, he built 121 rest houses to serve travelers that were located every fifteen kilometers, as well as more than one hundred hospitals and many architecturally stunning temples, including two dedicated to the King's parents.

Queen Indradevi was also highly skilled at managing state affairs while her husband was away at war. Indeed, she was a polymath whose multidimensional skills included poetry. In 1916, a giant stone slab was discovered on the grounds of an ancient temple carved with an epic poem composed by Queen Indradevi. The slab was once covered in gold, and scholars agree that the poem's author, Indradevi, had a flawless command of Sanskrit and the use of the language's demanding structures in the composition of poems. There was also the discovery of carvings depicting Queen Jayarajadevi and Queen Indradevi teaching groups of students in Buddhism. The fact that these two women of the twelfth century were acknowledged for their academic wisdom is eye-opening.

Queen Jayarajadevi, Queen Indradevi, and King Jayavarman VII ushered in the Golden Age of ancient Cambodia. They were socially progressive rulers who instigated massive building projects, including some of the most stunning Buddhist temples ever built.

Benazir Bhutto—Inspiration for Muslim Female Leaders

On December 27, 2007, Benazir Bhutto was traveling in a motorcade surrounded by thousands of supporters after returning to Pakistan following an exile of seven years; she was poised to run for the Pakistani congress. Tragically, she was hit by a suicide assassin's bullet on that day. Bhutto was rushed to the hospital, but she had lost so much blood that she died upon arrival.

Bhutto was a charismatic and controversial political figure who made a lasting impression on the world stage. When she was voted in as Prime Minister of Pakistan by an overwhelming majority in 1988, she was seen as a beacon for all women, both Muslim and non-Muslim, around the world. From her rise in politics to her death, her life was marked by a tumultuous legacy. Perhaps she was judged unfairly by those opposed to female rulers, as has often been the case throughout history, or perhaps Benazir Bhutto was no different from any other politician: a mixture of good and bad.

Benazir Bhutto was well-educated, and although many pundits have accused her of being a rich and privileged scion of an elite political dynasty, she truly wanted to help and to be loved by the people. Her father, Zulfikar Ali Bhutto, was a staunch advocate of gender equality who always made her feel she could accomplish anything. Benazir traveled with her father on a few of his official political visits with other world leaders, and at age sixteen, she met Indira Gandhi.

The story of Benazir Bhutto's rise to power begins when her father became the prime minister of Pakistan in 1973. Then, in 1979, military dictator General Zia Ul Haq seized power, and her father was imprisoned. Then a young adult, Benazir Bhutto had been studying law at Oxford University and had just returned to Pakistan. Within a few days of her arrival, her beloved father was executed. She and other members of her family were detained repeatedly over the next few years.

Her worst experience was in 1981, when she was sent to a desert prison at Sukkur where she was held in solitary confinement for six months during the intense summer heat. She suffered from incessant insect bites and became so ill that when finally released, she had to spend several months in the hospital. In 1984, she and her two brothers were permitted to leave the country and settled in London, where they started an underground movement to fight against the dictatorship of General Zia.

In 1985, there was widespread dissent against Zia's government, and Bhutto was elected along with her mother to co-chair the Pakistan's People's Party, which her father had founded. Upon returning to her country, she received a thunderous welcome. Benazir Bhutto married Asif Ali Zardari in 1987. One year later, when free elections were finally held, she became Pakistan's prime minister at thirty-five, one of the youngest heads of state anywhere and the first woman ever to be prime minister of a Muslim country.

While in office, she brought electricity to the countryside and built many schools across the country. She also prioritized ending hunger and providing housing and health care, while also making plans to modernize Pakistan. Bhutto also had many aspirations to help her people—and particularly women—to live fulfilling lives in a heavily patriarchal society.

Unfortunately, her terms in office were marked by one obstacle after another. During her first term, the conservative opposition accused her government of being corrupt, and she was ousted after only twenty-two months in office. However, the interim government was also charged with corruption, and Benazir Bhutto was reelected as prime minister in 1993. Nevertheless, Bhutto faced constant opposition from the Islamic fundamentalist movement. Then her brother Murtaza Bhutto, who was living abroad, returned to Pakistan, where he accused his sister and her husband, Asif Ali Zardari, of corruption. In a startling turn of events, Murtaza was killed in a gunfight, along with his bodyguard. This shocked everyone, and the Pakistan People's Party was divided over accusations of corruption and support for Bhutto and her husband.

In 1996, Bhutto was once again ousted based on allegations of mismanagement. Bhutto's husband was imprisoned, and again, she was forced to leave her homeland. For nine years, she and her children lived in exile in London, during which her husband remained behind bars. Despite the many tragedies she endured, Bhutto continued to advocate for democracy in her country. In 2004, her husband was at last released and rejoined his family in the UK.

In 2007, as the political pendulum in Pakistan was swinging back toward free elections and the Pakistan People's Party regained ground, Bhutto felt that there was a very good chance of her being reelected. She and her husband returned to enthusiastic crowds, but on December 27, while she was campaigning in Rawalpindi, a suicide bomber fired shots at her and then detonated a bomb. She was rushed to the hospital but did not survive. More than twenty other people also died that day.

The assassination of the country's most popular democratic leader caused mass riots. In 2008, the People's Party in Pakistan easily won. Benazir's son, Bilawal Bhutto Zardari, was appointed to head the party, even though he was only nineteen. Eventually, Benazir's husband, Asif Ali Zardari, entered politics. Both father and son still hold offices within the Pakistan government as of 2024.

Her career has been celebrated as a triumph for women in the Muslim world and the global fight against Islamic extremism. At the same time, she has been accused of corruption and bad governance. Her efforts and struggle to champion democracy remain a deeply respected and lasting legacy. Several universities and public buildings in Pakistan bear Benazir Bhutto's name.

Corazon Aquino—the Reluctant President

Corazon (Cory) Aquino never planned on being president. Her husband Ninoy Aquino was the politician in the family and a strong dissenting voice during the dictatorship of Ferdinand Marcos.

While Ninoy Aquino campaigned and traveled, Cory preferred to stay behind the scenes. She was naturally shy and didn't want to be on the stage with her husband. Despite her shyness, she was a gracious hostess for their many political gatherings and dedicated her time and energy to raising their five children.

Ninoy became a senator and then the governor of Tarlac province. He stood solidly against the authoritarianism of Marcos. When martial law was implemented in 1972, Ninoy and other opposition members were incarcerated.

Corazon Aquino had to carry the burden of raising their children alone for the next seven years while her husband was imprisoned. Even while in jail, Ninoy was able to rally political activism, and the shy Cory dutifully delivered Ninoy's speeches to the people.

Due to Ninoy's health difficulties while in prison, President Carter petitioned for the Aquino family to be able to go to the US for treatment. Fortunately, they were able to take refuge in Massachusetts for the next five years. Cory treasured their time spent in Boston away from politics. However, when Ninoy recovered from his illness, he could not give up his desire to depose Marcos. Despite warnings not to return, Ninoy headed back to the Philippines in 1983 and was assassinated.

Overnight, the shy and quiet Cory was pushed into the limelight. Somehow she found the strength and courage to carry on her husband's mandate. When millions of Filipinos filled the streets of Manila, the dignity with which Cory led the procession despite her immense grief left an indelible impression. She emerged as the central figure in the anti-Marcos movement, which came to be known as "People Power."

Ferdinand Marcos became very concerned about the mass demonstrations against his regime and called for new presidential elections in February of 1986. He mistakenly gambled on the belief that there was still broad public support for him. His hubris prevented him from fully recognizing the power of Corazon Aquino. Marcos was known to have publicly slighted her by saying, "She's just a woman, and her proper place is in the bedroom."

When the election results came in, it was obvious that Aquino had won by a landslide. But Marcos wasn't about to relinquish his dictatorship. He pressured the parliament to declare him the winner. Four days of chaotic and violent popular protest followed, and many top military leaders defected to Corazon Aquino's side. Ferdinand Marcos and his wife Imelda were forced to flee and took exile in the US.

On February 25, 1986, due to the "People Power Revolution," Corazon Aquino became the eleventh president of the Philippines and the first woman to win this position. She restored democracy to the country and instated a new constitution, serving as president until 1992. More than a decade later, her son, Benigno Aquino III, would become the fifteenth president of the Philippines.

As a grief-stricken widow and mother of five, the power of Corazon Aquino's leadership wrested autocratic control from a strongman. Her courage and unwavering devotion to the cause of democracy have earned her a place in world history.

Megawati Sukarnoputri—the Daughter Who Would Be President

To fully appreciate Megawati Sukarnoputri (a surname meaning "daughter of Sukarno"), we should remember that the Dutch colonized Indonesia for hundreds of years, during which many indigenous peoples perished; then, after Indonesia won its independence from 1945 to

1965, a homegrown tyrant emerged and imposed dictatorship upon the country.

Megawati's father was Sukarno, the founding father of Indonesia, which prior to its independence was known as the Dutch East Indies. He ushered in the promise of peace and prosperity through socialistic reforms but was ultimately betrayed by his chief of staff, General Suharto. In 1965, the Indonesian Communist Party attempted to take power via a coup; General Suharto crushed the opposition, took control through military force, and placed President Sukarno under house arrest. Megawati was in college at that time but left school and returned home to be with her father. Sukarno died of kidney failure in 1970.

After her father's death, Megawati Sukarnoputri and her family suffered a long period of hardship, as did the rest of the populace under Suharto's rule. When Suharto took power, a bloodbath followed as the army, with the help of private militias, slaughtered at least 500,000 alleged leftists and detained around a million more. Suharto imposed his authoritarian rule for the next thirty-two years.

During those dark times, Sukarnoputri kept her head above water and gained a reputation for being courageous and compassionate. She opened a small flower shop and spent much of her time and her hard-earned money to help the less fortunate. Even though she was the daughter of a former president, she led a simple and modest life. Her first husband had died in a plane crash when she was pregnant with their child. A few years later, she married her second husband, Taufiq Keimas, who encouraged her to enter politics and join the fledgling opposition party to Suharto's tyrannical government. In 1987, at age forty, she won a seat in parliament in opposition to Suharto. She successfully ran as a candidate of the Indonesian Democratic Party (PDI-P), later becoming its leader in 1993. However, change still didn't come for several years until an economic crisis highlighted Suharto's extreme wealth and corruption and the populace was totally fed up. There was an uprising, and massive riots led by students erupted across Indonesia. In 1998, Suharto at last resigned.

Sukarnoputri and her supporters were vying for her to become the next president. She was a rallying point and the hope of the opposition to Suharto's dictatorship. Her personal magnetism, combined with her father's legacy, assembled the largest crowds and demonstrations in Indonesian history. Finally, in 2001, she won and became the fifth president of Indonesia and its first woman president. Megawati served one term but has remained the head of the Council of Asian Liberals and Democrats and a constant voice for democracy.

Now, over two decades after her presidency, at age seventy-five, Megawati Sukarnoputri is still one of Indonesia's most influential female political personalities.

President Tsai Ing-wen—Shy Yet Powerful

Tsai Ing-wen has the distinction of having become the first female president of Taiwan, not through being associated with a political dynasty but by a vote of the people. Unlike others, she did not get into government due to the death of her spouse or through a military coup. She ascended to the highest office in government due to her own merits and smarts, and was reelected for a second consecutive term. It is also wonderful to note that she is a die-hard cat lady as well as a dog lover who featured her animal friends prominently during her election campaigns. She never dreamed that she would become president; growing up, she wanted to study ancient history because, as she humorously stated, "I wanted a quiet life. I thought I would become a historian or an archaeologist to study things that happened in the past [because] people that are dead already wouldn't jump up and argue with you."

Instead of digging up antiquities, Tsai earned a law degree from Cornell University and then attained a PhD from the London School of Economics. Later, she was a professor at two universities in Taiwan.

Tsai comes from a family of eleven children. Her father is a successful self-made entrepreneur who built a thriving transportation business. Her family background includes Hakka ancestry and grandparents who were part of the indigenous tribes of Taiwan. She is the first president of Taiwan to have that ancestral distinction. Although Tsai was a relative latecomer to politics, having joined the Democratic Progressive Party at age forty-eight, she quickly rose to become the chairperson of her party. She ran for the presidency in 2012 and failed; but in 2016, she won, and then won again in 2018.

Time magazine included President Tsai on their list of the most influential people in 2020, and in 2021, *Forbes* ranked her among the most powerful women in the world, close behind then Vice President Kamala Harris. She also garnered high praise for her skillful handling of the COVID-19 pandemic, during which the island nation experienced very low death rates. She has also been very popular with the younger generation for implementing progressive legislation securing same-sex marriage and transgender rights. She has crafted legislation to recognize the rich cultural heritage of the aboriginal tribes of Taiwan and protect their languages and customs. Tsai has also sought to revitalize economic growth, address social inequality, launch prison reforms, and tackle the climate crisis with renewable energy options.

Tsai combined liberal, compassionate qualities with hardline tactics to stand up to China's constant bullying. Unlike her predecessor, who tried to negotiate with China, she boosted Taiwan's military capabilities and aligned the nation with strategic partners such as the US and other countries in the region.

Before stepping down as president, Tsai invited Taiwanese American drag queen and dressmaker Nymphia Wind, the winner of Season 16 of the TV show *RuPaul's Drag Race*, to perform at the presidential office.

In May 2024, the presidency passed to Lai Ching-te. It is too soon to judge Tsai's legacy, but it is apparent that she has infused Taiwan's democratic movement with fresh and relevant processes that are engaging young participants who are vital to the future of Taiwan and the world.

CHAPTER TWO

AMAZING STRENGTH— MAVERICK WARRIORS AND FREEDOM FIGHTERS

The image of a fierce woman warrior charging into battle on her mighty steed with her sword shimmering in the sun has captivated the psyche of countless people, regardless of where they are from and whether they are female or male. Stories of Amazon-like women who could fight better than any man abound from the vast Steppes of Central Asia to the high, misty mountains of Cathay. But are such legends only fairy tales spun by fanciful storytellers, or is there truth to the mythic stories of powerful females who defy our stereotypes of the "fairer" sex?

Interestingly, contemporary archaeological discoveries and modern DNA techniques are beginning to validate the legends of brilliant sheroes who charged fearlessly into conflicts armed with both beauty and might.

Burial mounds (known as *kofun*) dating back to the first century in ancient Japan reveal that high-ranking females participated in the battles and governance of Yamatai, including Queen Himiko from Chapter One. Another spectacular unearthing of a royal tomb revealed Fu Hao, the warrior-queen of the Shang Dynasty.

Of course, not all wars are fought with weapons. In this chapter, we will meet both formidable females who courageously fought physical battles and others who fought with their unwavering will and determination despite overwhelming challenges, such as imprisonment, torture, and starvation.

Fu Hao—Ancient High Priestess and Commander

In 1976, a lavish tomb was discovered in Anyang in the Henan Province of China. The excavations revealed the extraordinary life of Fu Hao, one of the primary wives of King Wu Ding of the Shang Dynasty.

Fu Hao, also known as Lady Hao, was not only the royal consort of a powerful emperor but also a military commander, landowner, administrator, and high priestess. In short, she was one of the most extraordinary women of the ancient world.

The Shang Dynasty, which lasted from 1600 to 1046 BCE, is the earliest ruling dynasty to be recorded in writing, thanks to the technique of chiseled carving on animal bones, known as oracle or "dragon" bones. Knowledge gained by deciphering oracle bones combined with the discovery of Fu Hao's tomb in 1976 has provided definitive proof of the existence of this woman warrior who lived over 3,000 years ago. The

Shang Dynasty heralded the Bronze Age in China and was known for advances in math, astronomy, artwork, and military technology.

From the bone inscriptions, we know that Lady Hao played a commanding role during the reign of King Wu Ding, who ruled for six decades and had fifty-four wives. She led several significant military campaigns and was in charge of over 13,000 troops, of whom 600 were female.

The contents of her tomb, including an inventory of magnificent precious objects and weapons along with sacrificial offerings, clearly demonstrate the power and respect that Fu Hao garnered while she was alive. There were 1,600 objects, many of which were beautifully cast bronze vessels, ornate jade jewelry, and intricately made implements for sacrificial use, indicating that Fu Hao also held the position of a high priestess.

The Trung Sisters—Brave Rebels Against Colonization

Every year, on the sixth day of the second lunar month, the inhabitants of Hanoi visit the Hai Ba Trung Temple. They bring fresh flowers, food offerings, and prayers as burning incense fills the air with the heady scents of frankincense, cinnamon, cedar, and cloves. This commemoration has been going on year after year without fail for generations. 2022 marked the 1,982nd anniversary of this observance! Isn't that incredible? What persons or events could cause such devotion to endure for nearly two thousand years?

These devotions are a commemoration of the heroic actions of two sisters who fought for their country's independence from a dominating force of invaders that sought to eradicate their indigenous cultures. These two sisters also overcame patriarchal prejudices regarding the ability of women to wield military might and hold political power; they even brought together a formidable army of 80,000 volunteer fighters led by female generals, one of whom was none other than their own mother!

The Trung sisters, who were known to ride elephants into battle, and their rebel band successfully drove the Chinese out of Vietnam. It is recorded that a hated and corrupt Chinese overlord named Su Ding, who had executed the husband of one of the Trung sisters, was so terrified by this army led by women that he shaved his beard, cut his hair, disguised himself as a beggar, and fled back to the safety of the Han government in China. In just over a year, starting in 40 CE, the sisters and their army liberated sixty-five villages and dismantled fortresses built by the Chinese.

Of course, the Chinese emperor wasn't about to let two women humiliate him. He eventually responded with an overwhelming force led by one of his most ferocious generals, and they attacked by land and sea. Eventually, the sheer military size of the Han Dynasty was too much for the Trung sisters and their contingent. They were outnumbered by forces with more and better weaponry. Before the rising of the second full moon in 43 CE, the Trung sisters were cornered in an area around the Hat Giang River located just north of Hanoi. Rather than allowing themselves to be captured, the Trung sisters chose the traditional Vietnamese alternative in order to maintain their dignity: they departed by suicide. Many believe that they drowned themselves in the river, while others lean toward believing the popular folklore, which states that they disappeared into the clouds.

Triệu Thi Trinh—Following in the Footsteps of Her Sheroes

Some two hundred years after the death of the Trung sisters, another female rebel came to the fore to lead Vietnam out of the control of its occupiers.

Triệu Thị Trinh appeared at a time when the Chinese had subjugated Vietnam for nearly five centuries. The rule of the Wu Dynasty was particularly harsh and unjust. The Vietnamese population was heavily taxed and exploited. Thousands of skilled Vietnamese artisans were taken from their homeland to help build the new capital, Jianye, which would eventually become Nanjing. Tens of thousands of Viet people were killed by the Chinese when they dared to rebel.

Orphaned young, Triệu grew up with her brother, Triệu Quoc Dat, in an era of turmoil while living under intense Chinese suppression. When asked about her future plans as a child, she said, "I want to grow up and fight the enemies like Trung Trac and Trung Nhi [i.e., the Trung sisters]!"

Here is the story of a young woman who wasn't going to put up with maltreatment. Her sister-in-law was cruel, overbearing, and physically abusive. One day, she fought with her brother's sadistic wife, and in the heated tussle, killed her.

Due to this incident, Triệu left home at the age of nineteen. Instead of becoming overwhelmed and consumed with guilt, she channeled her energy into fighting against her people's oppression. She ventured deep into the forest and raised an army of over 1,000 rebels. Her brother heard news of his sister's unladylike activities and visited her mountain headquarters to plead with her to stop her warrior ways and get married.

She famously replied: "My wish is to ride the tempest, tame the waves, kill the sharks. I want to drive the enemy away to save our people. I will not resign myself to the usual lot of women who bow their heads and become concubines." Her indomitable spirit impressed him so much that he joined her in the fight.

Records from the Wu Dynasty make no mention of a renegade female commander winning battles against their well-trained and well-armed soldiers, most likely because they did not want to be shamed by having been defeated by a woman.

Her army fought the Chinese forces both as guerrillas in the jungle and in open field actions against walled cities. Legend says Triệu led her army into battle wearing golden armor, brandishing a sword in each hand, and riding a war elephant like the Trung sisters.

Lady Triệu led her army north from the Cu-Phong District to engage the Chinese, and before she turned twenty-three, defeated the Wu forces in more than thirty battles. Eventually, the sheer force of the Chinese army made it impossible for Lady Triệu and her army to keep fighting. And like the Trung sisters, Triệu chose to take her own life rather than face humiliation at the hands of the Chinese.

The Trung sisters and Lady Triệu continued to be symbols of courage during the fight for independence from France's colonial rule from the late 1800s until the 1950s, as well as decades later during the Vietnam War of the 1970s.

There is even a popular lullaby that is still sung today:

Sleep, sleep tight my child
So that I can fetch water to wash the gilded saddle of the elephant

Climb the hill if you want to see
General Lady Triệu on her golden gilded seat

Tomoe Gozen—the First Female Samurai

When it comes to fighting with swords, the samurais of Japan draw the most vivid picture of well-disciplined men wielding incredibly sharp blades of polished steel and slicing up their opponents with silent and deadly precision. It is extremely thought-provoking, then, to note that a woman was one of the major people who played a significant role in ushering in the Age of the Samurai.

Women warriors were not a rarity in medieval Japan. Due to the feudal nature of society during that era, there were constant clashes between powerful clans, and the entire family, including women and children, was trained to defend the castle. Indeed, being skilled in martial arts, including archery and horsemanship, was necessary for survival and protecting family wealth.

Two types of female samurais arose: the *onna-musha* and the *onna-bugeisha*. The former refers to a female offensive combatant trained to fight on the field, and the latter refers to a female warrior trained to defend the keep.

The end of the twelfth century in Japan was extremely turbulent and violent, culminating in the Genpei War, which lasted from 1180 to 1185. It was a bloody feud between the aristocratic Taira clan and the somewhat less aristocratic but very militant Minamoto clan for control of the country. Amidst the chaos and violence, Tomoe Gozen shines bright as the first female samurai. She not only turned heads with her beauty and charisma but also managed to chop off quite a few. (The taking of enemy heads was an important part of samurai culture. More heads cut off meant more respect and rewards.)

Historically, Tomoe is acknowledged as the concubine of Lord Kiso no Yoshinaka, a key player in the Minamoto clan. He was not only enamored of her feminine charms but also so impressed by her amazing warrior skills that he appointed her his leading commander in the Genpei War.

Here is an official account from *The Tales of Heike*:

Kiso no Yoshinaka had brought with him from Shinano two female attendants, Tomoe and Yamabuki. Yamabuki had fallen ill and stayed in the capital. Of the two, Tomoe was especially beautiful, with white skin, long hair, and charming features. She was also a remarkably strong archer, and as a swordswoman, she was a warrior worth a thousand, ready to confront a demon or god, mounted or on foot. She handled unbroken horses with superb skill; she rode unscathed down perilous descents. Whenever a battle was imminent, Yoshinaka sent her out as his first captain, equipped with strong armor, an oversized sword, and a mighty bow, and she performed more deeds of valor than any of his other warriors. Thus, she was now one of the seven who remained after all the others had fled or perished.

Unfortunately, members of the Minamoto clan were also vying for power amongst themselves to rule Japan, and Kiso no Yoshinaka's cousin, Minamoto no Yorinori, unleashed a fury of soldiers against Kiso and Tomoe. During the battle of Awazu, it became apparent that Yoshinaka would be defeated, and he commanded Tomoe to quit the field in order to save her life. However, Tomoe wasn't going to ride off without showing her devotion. As a last salute to her lover and master, she galloped full speed toward a band of thirty samurais from the opposition and headed straight for Onda no Hachiro, who was known for being an extremely strong man, and quickly decapitated him. His was the last head she would take.

After this spectacular display of Tomoe's martial skills, valor, and undying love, we are unsure what became of her. Many rumors have circulated throughout the centuries; one places her in a monastery where she recited prayers and mantras for the souls she had taken until her own death at the ripe old age of ninety.

Hangaku Gozen—Protector of the Keep

Another female warrior who has become legendary in Japan was a contemporary of Tomoe. Her real name is unknown, but historians named her Hangaku Gozen. While Tomoe was on the side of the Minamoto clan, Hangaku was allied with the Taira contingent.

Unlike Tomoe, who rode into battles as a combatant, Hangaku was an *onna-bugeisha*, a female warrior trained to defend the castle. From an early age, her father recognized her exceptional skills and placed a great deal of trust and responsibility on her shoulders.

During a three-month siege by the Minamoto army, Hangaku bravely defended their castle even though they were vastly outnumbered and provisions were running out. Dressed as a boy, Hangaku stood on the castle's highest tower and unleashed her deadly arrows one by one. Every single shot pierced attackers either in the head or through the chest. She was finally brought down when an enemy arrow punctured her thigh.

She was taken as a prisoner of war and presented to Shogun Minamoto no Yoriiye. Upon seeing her, he was known to have uttered, "Fearless as a man and beautiful as a flower."

It would have been a customary display of honor for Hangaku to have committed ritual suicide, but she was prevented from doing so by order of the Shogun. Instead of death by *seppuku*, Hangaku was given in marriage to one of Yoriiye's retainers, Asati Yoshito. It was believed that they wanted Hangaku to bear children who would be as brave and strong as she. It seems the union was a good match, and Hangaku gave birth to a son. From this point, records of her life become obscured.

Nakano Takeko—the Last Female Samurai

The waning years of the nineteenth century saw the end of the Age of the Samurai. Nakano Takeko fought in one of the last battles between the supporters of the Tokugawa Shogunate and the new political players who would usher in the Meiji Restoration, bringing power back into the hands of the imperial court.

Nakano was not only a remarkable female samurai; she is generally recognized as one of the last samurais, marking the end of their more than 600-year reign in Japan.

Nakano Takeko hailed from a famous samurai family and was trained from a tender age by her father, Nakano Heinai, and other accomplished warriors. She was so good that she taught other women how to fight using the *naginata* (a traditional polearm used by *onna-bugeisha*) and formed an all-female brigade that included other illustrious women warriors.

Nakano and her family relocated to Aizu, which was the last stronghold of the samurais against the Western-backed Meiji regime. Although she knew that it was a losing battle, Nakano organized a group of female warriors called the *Jōshitai*. Her forty-year-old mother, her sixteen-year-old sister, and several other women also joined in.

Reports say that she and her female defenders went into battle on a cold morning with heavy rain and sleet. Despite the harsh conditions, they did not waver in their resolve to fight off the soldiers from the Meiji Restoration. The men were initially surprised to encounter an all-female contingent and held their fire, at which point Nakano and her warriors took advantage. Nakano slew several enemies before she was shot. Knowing that she was going to die, Nakano asked her sister to cut off her head so that the enemy could not defile her spirit. Her sister, Yuko, did as she was told, and Nakano's head was taken to a temple and buried there. She was only twenty-one years old.

After her demise, Japan entered the period of the Meiji Restoration. The country reverted to imperial rule; with influence from the West, Japan eventually introduced more democratic governance. However, the Age of the Samurai lives on. Aside from the heavy emphasis on slashing and beheading, the seven noble virtues (Righteousness, Loyalty, Honor, Respect, Honesty, Courage, and Consistency) of these bygone warriors, known as *bushido*, are still followed by modern students.

The undying spirit of female warriors lives on vividly today as their stories are reimagined in anime, video games, movies, books, and manga.

Malahayati—the First Acknowledged Female Admiral

Nutmeg, cloves, and pepper have become so common in our kitchens that we forget these culinary spices were once very exotic and expensive commodities. Wars ignited between several European countries, including Spain, Portugal, and Holland, as various factions attempted to control the spice trade. The quest for dominance of these rich flavor enhancers also made it imperative for the indigenous peoples living on the spice islands to defend their territories and natural wealth against invaders.

Keumalahayati, also known as Malahayati, was the first recognized female admiral in the world. She bravely defended the Kingdom of Aceh (located in modern-day Indonesia) against the Dutch and Portuguese with her brilliant naval maneuvers and negotiating skills.

In 1599, the Dutch came barging into the country uninvited with a fleet commanded by de Houten and the intention of making off with Aceh's resources. However, Malahayati put a quick stop to this unprovoked aggression by boarding the enemy's ship and killing one of their commanders.

Malahayati also formed an army of over 2,000 women, all widows of soldiers who had died. This incredible all-female fighting force was integral to Malahayati's success in defending the seas from Western aggression.

Her reputation as the guardian of land and sea was so great that the British, who also had a keen interest in trade, decided to use diplomatic means instead of military tactics to gain access to the Malacca Strait. In 1602, Queen Elizabeth of England sent an emissary to the Sultan of

Aceh; it was Malahayati who negotiated the terms with Britain. The agreement allowed the English access to the seas around Malacca, and soon after, they were able to build merchant offices in Banten, located in East Java.

Malahayati was eventually killed on an expedition against a Portuguese fleet. There are many institutions of learning and hospitals named in her honor. Some 400 years later, in 2020, the president of Indonesia declared her a national hero.

Gabriela Silang—the Bolo-Wielding Shero of Ilocos Sur

Ferdinand Magellan landed in the Philippines in 1521 and began the colonization of the islands. Few know that he was killed by a local chieftain named Lapulapu, that the indigenous peoples continuously fought for their freedom from Spain's imperial rule, and that many women were at the forefront of these rebellions. María Josefa Gabriela Cariño, also known as Gabriela Silang, is one shining example.

She was born in 1731 in the beautiful seacoast town of Santa in Ilocos Sur. Separated from her parents at a young age, she was raised by a Catholic priest. When she was old enough, he arranged for her to be wedded to a wealthy merchant many years her senior. Fortunately for the young and beautiful Gabriela, her spouse passed away after three years, freeing her from the arranged marriage.

Gabriela soon met the charismatic and highly intelligent rebel Diego Silang. They were immediately attracted to each other and quickly married in 1757. They were united not only by love, but also in their strong desire to free their province from the heavy yoke of the Spaniards, who extracted mineral wealth from the land, enslaved many locals, and imposed excessive taxation and payments of tribute. Spain also restricted Filipino religious rights and political sovereignty.

Despite repeated imprisonment, Diego Silang gathered a rebel force that was poised to fight for the freedom of the Filipino people. However, two of his closest friends betrayed him after being bribed by the Catholic Church, and one of them, Miquel Vicos, killed Diego in 1763, aged only thirty-two.

Gabriela Silang was devastated and had to flee to save her own life. After several months of grief, she courageously took on full leadership of the resistance. She moved into the Abra mountains to establish a new base and reassembled more than 2,000 fighters.

She famously said, "Women are not just objects to be kept in the kitchen; they too have the right to fight for their country's freedom." In the winter of 1763, she proved her mettle by successfully laying siege to the Spanish garrison at Vigan, the capital of Ilocos Sur. She and her troops held their position for four months and choked off Spanish supply lines, weakening the colonizers' control over the region.

The Spanish government retaliated with deadly force, and Gabriela was captured. She was led into Vigan and hung in front of a crowd of Spanish sympathizers. She, like Diego, was only thirty-two.

In recognition of her extraordinary contributions to Philippine history, Gabriela Silang has been honored in numerous ways. In 1991, the Philippine government declared her a national hero, and a statue of her was erected in her hometown of Santa, Ilocos Sur. Additionally, the Gabriela Silang Memorial Shrine was established in Vigan to commemorate her legacy and achievements.

An iconic image of the beautiful and strong Gabriela charging ahead on a horse, with her long hair dancing in the wind, wielding a bolo, perfectly encapsulates her bravery.

Lakshmi Bai—the Rani of Jhansi

Lakshmi Bai, born Marnikarnika Tambe, is one of India's national heroines. Raised in a household of boys, she was fearless and brilliant as a military strategist. When her husband, a *maharaja* (prince), died, she came out of *purdah* (seclusion) to fight the British, becoming the key figure extraordinaire who took special care in training women as skilled fighters for her army. These women came to be known as the "amazons of Jhansi." Lakshmi herself was famous for calmly taunting enemy generals by declaring, "Do your worst, I will make you a woman." Her fame spread like wildfire throughout India, making her their national shero, after she broke through an encircling ambush of British soldiers during battle and escaped on horseback to a rebel rendezvous point a hundred miles away in just twenty-four hours with a ten-year-old boy clinging to her back. She and the boy were the only two survivors of the slaughtered Indian troops. It should also be noted that Lakshmi was in full armor in the sweltering 120-degree heat. She died on the battlefield in Gwalior in 1858 when she was barely thirty; a British general called her the "greatest hero" he'd ever known.

Janaki Thevar—Lieutenant of an All-Female Army and Parliamentarian

"We may be the softer and fairer sex, but surely I protest against the word 'weaker.' All sorts of epithets have been given to us by man to guard his own selfish interests. It is time we shattered these chains of men along with the chain of Indian slavery." Having said words like that, you know the woman who spoke them was a force to behold!

Janaki Thevar was born in Malaya into a well-to-do Tamil family with roots in India. At the time of her birth, parts of Southeast Asia, including India, Burma (now Myanmar), Singapore, and Malaya (now Malaysia), were still under the colonial rule of the British Raj. Although she enjoyed a very comfortable home life, she wasn't going to sit back and follow the mundane path of her peers. She had the soul of a rebel and wanted to fight for freedom from the oppression of colonization and for gender equality.

Janaki Thevar was greatly inspired by the independence movement in India and donated her gold jewelry to the Indian National Army, which was actively fighting against the British. Then, against the strong objection of her family, Thevar joined the Rani Jhansi Regiment (RJR), an unprecedented force of over 500 women being trained to be warriors. This all-female army, named after the unforgettable Lakshmi Bai of Jhansi, was created during the start of World War II.

The RJR was not just a token regiment that involved young women in helping with the war effort. Daily drills included training on how to use rifles, machine guns, and grenades, night marches, and strenuous physical exercises. The training was tough, and living conditions were spartan. Despite the challenges, she proved her mettle and was soon promoted to lieutenant. Then, eighteen-year-old Janaki Thevar became the commander of the Burma contingent of the RJR.

In the months that followed, she and her regiment rescued wounded soldiers when the British bombed the Red Cross hospital in Rangoon. Later, when the Indian National Army was in retreat, she trekked through the dangerous swamps and jungles of Burma to bring fellow fighters back to safety.

The RJR disbanded when World War II ended. Eventually, India gained its independence from Britain in 1947, and Malaysia followed suit in 1957.

In 1948, Janaki Thevar married Athi Nahappan, the publisher of a daily newspaper; they eventually had three children. Not content with mere domesticity, she turned her attention to social justice issues and became one of the first to fight against child marriages in Malaysia. She was instrumental in organizations such as the Girl Guide Association and NGOs that serve women. Then, she became a senator in the upper house of the Malaysian Parliament.

Her tireless activism and achievements inspired the Indian government to honor her with the Padma Shri Award in 2000, the fourth-highest civilian award. She was the first woman living outside India to receive the honor. Janaki Thevar passed away from pneumonia in 2014 at the age of eighty-nine.

Amdaeng Muen—She Fought for Love

Amdaeng Muen's story is about a determined and brave young woman who did everything for love, and in her singular struggle, forever changed the fate of girls and women in the nation of Siam (modern Thailand).

She was born in a small village in Nonthaburi Province in 1845. At the time, there was enormous gender disparity, and a well-known Siamese saying that went, "Women are buffaloes, men are human," was often used to degrade women.

Siamese women had absolutely no rights and were not allowed to be educated. Very few learned how to read and write. Females were expected to do housekeeping, childbearing, and care for the family, while men could attend school, travel freely, and do as they pleased.

Amdaeng was naturally intelligent from an early age and had a healthy dose of curiosity. She begged the monks at a local Buddhist temple to allow her to learn how to read and write along with the boys. While studying at the temple, she met a young man named Rid, and they fell deeply in love.

When Amdaeng turned twenty-one, her parents sold her off to a wealthy man named Phu, who was many years older and already had several wives. She refused and ran away a few times. Her parents caught her, beat her, and kept her locked up. But she tried to flee again, and this time, she was arrested by the police. In jail, the prison guards, who were bribed by Phu, continued to beat and torture Amdaeng to force her into marrying the man she despised, but still she stubbornly refused.

Her sweetheart Rid came to her rescue and helped her escape; they immediately fled to Bangkok. Instead of hiding for fear of being caught, she headed straight to the Grand Palace and asked for an audience with the king! On December 10, 1865, she presented her petition before King Mongkut, and he was sympathetic to her plea. He issued a royal decree, pardoned her, and sent officials to investigate her case.

Eventually, the king ordered her parents to return the dowry from the wealthy Phu, and she was allowed to marry the man she truly loved. Her case further inspired the king to revise Siamese law and acknowledge women's rights in choosing their husbands and their fates. As a result, it also became illegal in Siam to sell a daughter or a wife.

As a side note, King Mongkut, also known as King Rama IV, is famous in his own right as the real-life inspiration for the famous musical *The King and I*. He advocated for the rights of women and freed many of his concubines.

Amdaeng Muen risked everything and fought against her family, the law, and centuries of gender bias with nothing except her wit, tenacity, and immense love. This was a young woman who knew what she wanted and went for it! In that journey, she also brought freedom to all women in Siam.

In 1939, the name by which Siam is known was changed to Thailand, which means "land of the free."

Qiu Jin—Revolutionary Poet and Feminist Martyr of China

In the three short decades of her life, Qiu Jin went from being a privileged daughter and then the wife of a wealthy merchant and mother of two children to a woman who abandoned her family, only to become a poet and feminist revolutionary who wasn't afraid to give her life up for her cause.

Qiu Jin was born into a prominent family. Unusual for the time, she was encouraged to study along with her brother. From an early age, it was apparent that she was very smart and strong-willed. Despite her relative freedom of education, she was still subjected to having her feet bound and forced to enter into an arranged marriage.

In 1895, she married a man chosen by her father and went on to have a son and daughter with him. A few years after their marriage, they moved from Shaoxing to Beijing, the capital of China. In Beijing, Qiu Jin saw firsthand the insidious corruption and decline of the Qing Dynasty: the poor and homeless lined the streets while wealthy foreigners reaped the profits of trade in opium and other illicit commerce. Qiu Jin fully understood that a revolution was needed for China to save itself from this invasion of foreigners and the internal festering of social and cultural decline. She connected with other female intellectuals and started a feminist newspaper.

Her home life became intolerable as she clearly saw that her husband was a self-centered man who indulged in drinking, gambled, and patronized brothels. In a supreme act of defiance against Confucian patriarchy, she unbound her feet and started to wear men's clothing. In 1904, Qiu Jin boldly decided to leave her family. She sold all her jewelry and boarded a boat for Japan, leaving her dullard husband and her beloved children behind.

She connected with other Chinese freethinkers and revolutionaries in Japan, including Dr. Sun Yat-Sen, who is known as "the father of modern China." Her alliance with other change makers crystallized her dedication to freeing China from the corruption and incompetency of the Qing Dynasty. She was also convinced that Chinese women had to free themselves from centuries of patriarchal oppression and join the revolution.

Qiu Jin returned to China in 1904 and founded the Datong Women's School, which trained girls to be independent thinkers and martial artists. The school was also a front for a secret plot to overthrow the Qing government. Unfortunately, their plot was compromised in 1907, and Qiu Jin was arrested and charged with sedition as an accomplice to the murder of a Qing official. She was found guilty and beheaded just two days after her arrest. She was only thirty-two years old.

Qiu Jin's death inspired many other women to fight for China's emancipation. The Qing Dynasty was finally overthrown in 1911, and Dr. Sun Yat-Sen became the provisional president of the new Chinese government. In 1912, Dr. Sun honored her with a formal funeral and named her the first female martyr of the revolution.

More than a century after her death, many Chinese still visit her tomb beside West Lake in Hangzhou to pay their respects to the woman now embedded in the national consciousness as a bold feminist heroine.

This poem, written by Qiu Jin when she left her family, best sums up her sacrifice.

Regrets: Lines Written En Route to Japan

Sun and moon have no light left, earth is dark,
Our women's world is sunk so deep, who can help us?
Jewelry sold to pay this trip across the seas,
Cut off from my family, I leave my native land.
Unbinding my feet, I clean out a thousand years of poison,
With heated heart arouse all women's spirits.
Alas, this delicate kerchief here,
Is half stained with blood, and half with tears.

Elizabeth Choy—Altruistic Shero of Singapore

This remarkable woman warrior did not fight with weapons. Instead, her physical and emotional fortitude in overcoming extreme torture while imprisoned and then having the generosity of heart to forgive her tormentors showed that she was tougher than any soldier fighting on the battlefield.

Choy was born in 1910 in Kudat, North Borneo, in what is today known as Sabah, Malaysia. She was the oldest of six siblings and was raised by their widowed mother. From an early age, Elizabeth excelled academically and was awarded the Prize of Honor by St. Margaret School when her family moved to Singapore. She had plans to attend college but had to give up her dreams of higher education when her mother passed away in 1931 during the height of the Great Depression. Instead of going to university, she got a job as a teacher, earning just enough to support her younger siblings and their education.

Although economically strapped and unable to attend university, Elizabeth became a knowledgeable and wise teacher. She eventually married Choy Khun Hong, who was an accountant. By no means well-off, they were leading a comfortable and simple life until the imperial expansion schemes of Emperor Hirohito caused Japan to occupy China and then continued its aggression into Singapore and the rest of Asia. In 1942, Japanese troops entered Singapore and declared martial law. Many intellectuals and dissidents were put in jail, and both Elizabeth and her husband lost their jobs.

They both started to work at the canteen in a local hospital; meanwhile, they secretly supplied food, medicine, money, letters, and even radios to British prisoners of war held by the Japanese military at Changi Prison.

Unfortunately, they were caught in a dragnet and thrown into the same prison. That is where Elizabeth really showed her unbendable spirit. An affidavit from her husband states, "Elizabeth was tied up with hands and legs to a frame kneeling on [a] wood fire. They took out two hot [pieces of] lead and applied them to her body for fifteen minutes. She was screaming all the time…"

Despite the unbearable pain, she never confessed or revealed any names of the prisoners they had helped. Even her captors were struck by her unbreakable will. Her torturers were so impressed by her inner strength that they described her as being courageous, selfless, and altruistic.

Elizabeth spent nearly 200 days in prison in conditions that would likely have broken the strongest man, but she never gave in. After the war, she was invited to England to recuperate. She was received in an audience with Queen Elizabeth and awarded the Order of the British Empire. She stayed in England for about four years and even posed for the famous sculptress Dora Gordine, who created two beautiful and regal statues of Choy. One is named "Flawless Crystal," and the second one is called "Jade."

True to her heroic and selfless nature, she continued her educational work when she returned to Singapore and became the first woman on the Legislative Council in 1951. She tirelessly campaigned for the poor and eventually founded a school for the blind. She passed away in 2006 at the age of ninety-six.

Annette Lu—from Jailed Dissident to Vice President

Annette Lu graduated from Harvard Law School and could have led a posh life as a corporate attorney. Instead, she followed her heart to stand up for democracy and gender equality in her native country of Taiwan, even though doing so landed her in jail for six years. While she was in prison, her mother passed away. Annette developed thyroid cancer but still managed to write her first novel using the wash basin as a table and toilet paper as her writing pad. From living through imprisonment as a dissident to becoming the first female vice president of Taiwan, Annette Lu exemplifies tenacity and courage.

Annette was born in 1946 in the northern city of Taoyuan; at the time, Taiwan was still a colony of Japan. When she was three years old, the nationalist government of China, led by General Chiang Kai-Shek, moved to Taipei after the communist takeover of China. Although Lu's family experienced financial hardship, she was bright and intelligent and easily sailed through her academic life, receiving scholarships along the way. She graduated from Taiwan National University in 1967 and then earned not one but *two* master's degrees in law from the University of Illinois in Urbana-Champaign (1971) and Harvard University (1978). Her stellar academic achievements gave no hint of her future activism against the martial law decreed by Chiang under the Kuomintang (KMT) government.

Upon her return to Taiwan, she became disenchanted with the authoritarian rule of the Kuomintang and its patriarchal approach and established herself as a feminist activist. She wrote a book entitled *New Feminism* and joined the Tangwai Movement, which advocated for democracy and open elections. In 1979, on International Human Rights Day, she gave a passionate and rousing twenty-minute speech severely criticizing the government to a large audience. After the rally, Annette, along with other members of the Tangwai Movement, was arrested and tried for "violent sedition" by a military court; she was given a prison sentence of twelve years. Due to the help of Amnesty International and others, she was released after about six years.

In the decades after being released from jail, Annette continued to fight for democracy and gender parity, working as a lawyer, journalist, and academic. In 2000, Chen Shui-bian, Annette Lu, and the Democratic Progressive Party made history by toppling the monopoly on power held by the KMT, which had ruled Taiwan for over fifty years. Chen Shui-bian and Lu became their country's first Taiwan-born president and vice president.

Due to her resolute activism, she was elected vice president of Taiwan for two consecutive terms. Her primary areas of focus were promoting human rights, environmental protection, fostering technological development, and foreign affairs.

Although Annette Lu is now retired from government, she continues to be a dynamic doyenne of Taiwan's political and social issues. She also continues to write novels and commentaries.

CHAPTER THREE

BRAINS UNLEASHED— TRAILBLAZING WOMEN IN SCIENCE AND MEDICINE

In every country and throughout history, girls were deprived of science and mathematics education. Claims were made that there are biological differences between boys and girls that made it impossible for females to study and grasp the complex mathematical and technical complexities inherent in the scientific disciplines. And for Asian girls and women, the combination of male bias coupled with racial prejudice means that they face a "double bind": a term used for the situation of women of color who experience both sexism and racism. There is also a tendency to view Asian women as being quiet and passive; therefore, when they show their assertiveness and intelligence, especially in science, they have to overcome layers of stereotyping, even from within their own ethnic communities.

Despite all these challenges, Asian female geniuses have risen again and again to prove that the oppressive gravity of narrow-mindedness cannot weigh down brilliance. Women doctors, physicists, biochemists, and women in many more disciplines are paving the way for a better future that includes females and males of all ethnic backgrounds working together as equals to untangle our problems in the modern Anthropocene Age and to probe the mysteries of the universe.

Dr. Anandibai Gopal Joshee—from Child Bride to Honored Physician

Anandibai Joshee lived a very short life, yet one that was genuinely extraordinary. She was a child bride who was given at the tender age of nine to a man almost twenty years her senior. When she was fourteen, she gave birth to a son, but he only lived for ten days. This unfortunate fate ignited her interest in learning about premature infant death and women's health.

Fortunately for Anandibai Joshee, her husband was a progressive thinker from the Brahmin caste who supported her education and even encouraged her to learn English. The combination of inherent intelligence and this support from her husband, along with help from American missionaries, enabled her to travel to the US and enter the Women's Medical College of Pennsylvania. She was the first woman from India to receive a medical degree from America, which she achieved in 1886 at age twenty-one, despite difficulties with her health in the cold American climate.

Dr. Joshee's accomplishment was widely celebrated; even Queen Victoria of England sent her a congratulatory letter when she graduated from medical college. Anandibai Joshee received a hero's welcome upon her return to India and was immediately appointed to be the physician-in-charge of the female ward at the prestigious Albert Edward Hospital in Kolhapur. In an unfortunate irony, Dr. Joshee's intense will and her dedication to becoming a physician took a heavy toll on her health, and she died from complications of tuberculosis at twenty-two. The entire country mourned her passing.

Dr. Anandibai Joshee's path to becoming a physician inspired countless Indian women to pursue careers in medicine. Traditional gender barriers could not impede her deep desire to improve the health of children and women. In 2016, the Government of India honored her with a commemorative stamp recognizing her impact on medicine and women's education. Many hospitals and medical institutions in India bear her name, reflecting her lasting influence as a pioneer of women's health in her country.

Dr. Margaret Chung—Multifaceted Maverick of Medicine

There is a black-and-white photo of the graduating class of 1916 from the University of Southern California's College of Physicians and Surgeons. In this image, there are four rows of students, all males, posing before the camera. Some are smiling broadly, a few have their faces turned nonchalantly at an angle, while others express the solemnity of their achievements with serious countenances.

One stands out because he is the only Asian graduate. His name was Mike Chung, and he is seen gazing directly at the camera with a slight furrow between his eyebrows, looking reserved—or perhaps it was a guarded, inward sense of pride at what he had achieved in an era of intense racial bias against the Chinese in America. Despite that bias and the fact that he had come from an impoverished family, Mike managed to graduate and become a doctor.

Life presents many improbable tales, and this is the story of a very intelligent, tenacious, and boundary-breaking individual who defied all odds. What is truly remarkable is that "Dr. Mike Chung" in the photograph is actually Dr. *Margaret* Chung, the first American-born Chinese woman to become a doctor in the US. During her medical studies, she had to dress as a man to deflect taunting from fellow male classmates.

From a young age, Margaret had wanted to be a surgeon. She would play pretend doctor and perform "surgery" by sewing the opened edges of banana peels together with a needle and thread. Since she was the oldest of eleven children from a family plagued by poverty, her chances of ever attending medical school were slim. The other factors of her being both Chinese and a woman made her dream seem concretely unreachable. But Margaret was not bothered by immovable obstacles, for she had a gift for repeatedly breaking down walls to reach her goals. She later worked her way through college after winning an *LA Times* scholarship and then went on to medical school.

After completing her medical residency at the Kankakee State Hospital in Illinois, in 1922, she moved from Hollywood to San Francisco and established herself in private practice in Chinatown. There she treated both the Chinese American population and non-Chinese locals, including famed performers Helen Hayes, Tallulah Bankhead, and Sophie Tucker. Incidentally, a romantic liaison blossomed between Sophie Tucker and Margaret Chung. Intent on protecting herself from damaging rumors about her sexuality, she traveled outside Chinatown to frequent the bars, speakeasies, and cafes that formed a growing queer subculture in San Francisco's North Beach neighborhood.

When the Japanese invaded China in 1937, many American pilots wanted to join the fight to support the Chinese. Since the United States did not enter the war until 1941, Dr. Chung became an important secret recruiting agent who helped those young Americans sympathetic to the Chinese cause join the good fight. The pilots she secretly recruited became part of the "Flying Tigers," a group of pilots trained in Burma under the Republic of China Air Force to help turn back the Japanese invasion of China prior to the United States formally joining World War II in 1942.

This alliance of young American soldiers and the medical maverick started when US Navy Reserves Ensign Steven Bancroft reached out to Dr. Chung to ask if she could help him get a commission in the Chinese military. She invited Bancroft and some of his pilot friends to her home in San Francisco for dinner, and they all immediately became fast friends.

Dr. Margaret Chung extended her hand as a humanitarian by adopting these pilots as de facto surrogate family members, nourishing them with regular dinners at her home. They ate together almost every night and went on companionable camping and hunting trips. They started to joke about how to describe their unusual bond. As she later recalled in her autobiography, one night, one of the pilots "spoke up and said, 'Gee, you are as understanding as a mother, and we are going to adopt you; but, hell, you are an old maid, and you haven't got a father for us.' Feeling facetious that night, I cracked back at them, 'Well, that makes you a lot of fair-haired bastards, doesn't it?' " The name stuck, and her band of "bastards" even came to include John Wayne and Ronald Reagan! She had one fair-haired "daughter": Amelia Earhart.

Throughout World War II, Dr. Chung supported her "sons" at the front by sending them letters and Christmas gifts and connecting them to each other. She even gave each of her adoptees a jade Buddha pendant to wear as a good luck charm and a way for them to identify each other as members of her extraordinary extended family. Her home was always a welcoming place where she hosted Saturday dinners. Her fame grew, and her adopted family received significant media coverage as an example of American patriotism. Although she never married or had children of her own, she became a matriarch for hundreds of young adults during a highly volatile time in world history. Her extraordinary accomplishments were further celebrated in a comic book. Yes, that's right. She had the distinction of being the protagonist of a graphic novel published in 1942.

As if all her efforts were not enough, Dr. Chung somehow carved out more time and energy to press for greater inclusion of women in the United States military. She was instrumental in the creation of the WAVES (Women Accepted for Volunteer Emergency Service), a reserve corps for women in the Navy. She drew on her connections to government officials and her network of adopted children to lobby behind the scenes. Sadly, although she succeeded in getting the WAVES established in 1942, she never received proper recognition for her role in its creation. Her repeated applications to join the corps were rejected because of her race and rumors about her sexuality.

She died from ovarian cancer in 1959 at the age of sixty-nine. The music that serenaded her passing was light opera followed by hymns, and her six pallbearers, all white men, included two admirals and the mayor of San Francisco. The gathering of those who came to mourn her featured celebrities, notable politicians, and hundreds of the sons she had "adopted." The wife of Admiral Nimitz recorded in her diary: "All creed[s], all colors, all types of people, rich and poor, came to pay their homage."

There is a saying that how a person dies reflects how they lived. If this is true, then Dr. Chung indeed lived an extraordinary and noble life.

Dr. Ogino Ginko—First Female MD in Japan

To fully appreciate the exceptional determination that Ogino Ginko had to become the first Western-trained female doctor in Japan, we need to realize that she was born in 1850, when Japan was still under the rule of the Tokugawa Shogunate, which was so highly patriarchal that under its rule, girls and women had no rights. Men, however, were free to engage in polygamy and patronize prostitutes without judgment. Since Ogino was from a wealthy traditional family, she was expected to submit to an arranged marriage, have children, and serve her husband for the rest of her life.

Her husband frequented prostitutes and contracted gonorrhea, which he passed on to her. (This was before the invention of antibiotics to treat such STDs.) Ogino suffered terribly from the infection, and on top of the humiliating circumstance of being infected with the disease by her husband, she also had to suffer the humiliation of dealing with male doctors who were utterly unsympathetic to the unique medical needs of women. It took her almost two years to recover, and she became infertile. While in the hospital, she connected with other women who were also suffering from such conditions and realized that Japanese women needed female doctors who could understand their situation.

She divorced her wayward husband, which was no easy thing to do at that time in Japan; her family was not at all supportive, and she was stigmatized by society. However, she was on a mission to become a doctor, and nothing was going to stop her! Even though Ogino Ginko was from a wealthy family, she had only received a basic education in Confucian orthodoxy, so she had to complete a general higher education degree before studying medicine. She moved to Tokyo, entered an all-female college, and graduated with top honors.

Finally, she was ready to study medicine but had to overcome many hurdles to be accepted into an all-male private medical academy. Her fellow students and even the teachers gave her a hard time, but she ignored their chauvinistic taunting and just carried on. She graduated in 1882; however, she had to take an exam before she could practice medicine, and this became another hurdle as she was repeatedly denied permission to take the exam. Convincing the board to authorize it required the intervention of Ishiguro Tadanori, a prominent doctor, as well as the influence of several of Ogino Ginko's high-ranking acquaintances, along with her own erudite arguments.

She proudly presented herself before a group of chauvinists and delivered the eloquent petition that women were "divinely" suited to practice medicine. She noted that there were precedents in ancient times, when female doctors served at the royal courts of both China and Japan. These respected healers treated the "secret parts of the female body," and they held to a solemn and sacred code in their work. She also believed that only a woman could understand and treat a woman's body, while rejecting notions that pregnancy and menstruation rendered a woman incapable of practicing medicine. Finally, the powers that be allowed her to take the exam, which she passed with flying colors.

At thirty-five, Dr. Ginko established the Ogino Hospital in Yushima, which specialized in obstetrics and gynecology, and her fame spread far and wide. She also served as a doctor at Meiji Gakuin University, an all-female school founded by missionaries. Her tenure there introduced her to the Christian church, and she converted to Christianity.

In 1890, she married a Protestant clergyman, Yukiyoshi Shitaka, who was almost twenty years younger than she was. He was a utopian visionary who wanted to establish a Christian community in a remote part of Hokkaido. To everyone's surprise, Dr. Ginko gave up her practice in 1894 to join her husband there. They also adopted a child, the daughter of her husband's sister, who had died during a complicated childbirth in which Dr. Ginko was the obstetrician. Sadly, her spouse Yukiyoshi died a few years after they moved to Hokkaido.

In 1906, when Ogino Ginko returned to Tokyo from Hokkaido, she was amazed and gratified at how many young women were interested in becoming doctors, just as she had. She never regained the fame and momentum she had worked so hard to achieve when she first established her hospital near Tokyo. Some in the women's emancipation movement have criticized her for her marriage at a time when she could have done so much to enhance women's health care. But perhaps being true to herself required her to do what she felt was right for her. Perhaps after achieving the near-impossible task of becoming the first female physician in Japan, Ogino also wanted to experience love and parenthood.

Dr. Ogino Ginko was certainly the main role model for another shero of medicine, Dr. Yayoi, who established the first all-female hospital in Japan in 1900.

Dr. Yoshioka Yayoi—Emancipating & Empowering

Yoshioka Yayoi was born in 1871. Her father was a doctor, and as a child, she assisted her father as he cared for other children in her village. This early exposure instilled in Yoshioka a sense of duty expressed in the wish to serve others through medicine. Yoshioka is famous for establishing the first medical clinic for women in Japan, and she was also a trailblazer in other ways, even by modern-day standards.

She was one of the first women in Japan to have a dual-career marriage, which was completely unheard of at that time for Japanese women. Her husband, a German language teacher, founded a language academy, and Yoshioka opened her medical clinic right across the street from his school. Not only did she challenge social conventions by establishing a career of her own, but their marriage was very happy and financially prosperous. Their home became a hub for young Tokyo women eager to establish their professional careers. In this supportive milieu, Yoshioka encouraged them to become more independent and to become doctors and scientists, just like herself and her role model, Dr. Ogino Ginko.

Dr. Yayoi was the founder and president of the Tokyo Women's Medical Institute (today, Tokyo Women's Medical University), where she educated more than 7,000 women doctors. In addition to her work as a physician and educator, she was very active in government organizations. In the 1930s, Dr. Yayoi participated in the suffrage movement and was also a keen supporter of sex education. Due to her tireless dedication and that of countless other suffragettes, Japanese women finally gained the right to vote in 1946.

After fifty years of teaching, in 1953, she retired as an educator in order to focus on her family. In 1955, she received the Fujin Bunka Sho, the highest award given to women in Japan. She died of pneumonia in 1959 at age eighty-eight, but before her death, she received several awards, including the Order of the Precious Crown and the Order of the Sacred Treasure. There is a memorial museum dedicated to her in Kakegawa, Shizuoka, Japan.

Dr. Fe Villanueva del Mundo—Ninety-Nine Years of Many Firsts

Fe was the fifth child out of eight siblings, four of whom died from childhood diseases. Her sister Elisa, who was especially close to Fe, had written in her journal that she wanted to become a doctor to help the poor when she grew up. Unfortunately, Elisa died from a stomach infection before her ninth birthday. After her death, Fe read Elisa's journal and decided to take her sister's place and become a doctor who would save lives.

Fe's energies were completely devoted to her studies. At age fifteen, she graduated from the University of the Philippines' College of Medicine with scores so high that the then president of the Philippines, Manuel Quezon, offered her a full scholarship to further her studies at any medical university she wanted to attend. So Fe applied and was accepted for a two-year research fellowship at Harvard, and in 1940, she headed for America.

Much to her surprise, when she arrived at the dorm, there were only men. And the men there were even more surprised to see a petite Asian woman enter their male sanctum. Perhaps due to her name and exceptionally high grades, it never occurred to the admissions board at Harvard that "he" was a "she." To Harvard's credit, they decided to accept Fe into their graduate research program based on her academic excellence. (It wasn't until 1945 that Harvard opened its doors to accepting women.) While in the US, she also earned a master's degree in bacteriology from the University of Boston.

Del Mundo could have stayed in the US and built a successful and lucrative career, but she returned to the Philippines just as World War II was looming. Although she was well aware of the risks, she had an unwavering desire to serve her country, especially children from poor communities.

When once more in the Philippines, del Mundo revolutionized medicine in her country by providing health care to thousands of poor families. She also made breakthroughs in immunization and the treatment of jaundice and even invented a low-cost incubator made from bamboo that can be used in rural areas without electricity. Notably, she was a strong advocate of family planning and population control despite her personal devotion to the Catholic faith.

Here's an awe-inspiring list of her many firsts:

- First woman to be accepted to a Harvard Medical School research fellowship

- In 1957, she founded the first pediatric care hospital in Quezon City, the Children's Medical Center. She sold her own home to obtain a loan to fund the hospital

- She was instrumental in developing the BRAT (banana, rice, apple, tea) protocol, a lifesaving diet designed to treat severe diarrhea in children

- She became the founder and the first director of North General Hospital (now the Jose R. Reyes Memorial Medical Center), and the first Filipina to head a government general hospital (1945)

- First Filipina to be certified by the American Board of Pediatrics as a Board Diplomate (1947)

- Founder and first president of the Philippine Medical Women's Association (1949–1954)

- Editor-in-chief of the groundbreaking Textbook of Pediatrics and Child Health (1976)

- Her clinical studies include 150 scientific papers covering a broad range of topics, from the measurements of 10,839 newborn babies to commonly missed childhood diseases and the symptoms and treatment of dengue fever, as well as immunization.

Fe del Mundo never married and dedicated her entire life and all her financial resources to the people of the Philippines. During the last decade of her life, she lived in a single room on the second floor of her hospital, and she cared for patients until her last days. She passed away in 2011 at the age of ninety-nine and was posthumously awarded the Grand Collar of the Order of the Golden Heart Award by President Aquino that same year.

Chien-Shiung Wu—the First Lady of Physics

When twenty-four-year-old Chien-Shiung Wu sailed away from Shanghai harbor to the US, she did not know that it was the last time she would ever see her beloved parents or her generous uncle, who had funded her journey to America to study atomic physics. Nor could she anticipate that she would become a national superhero in China, revered for her indelible contribution to physics through her earth-shattering experiments into beta decay and parity. Wu forever changed how scientists and ordinary folks understand the nature of parity and showed us that the world is asymmetrical.

It was very fortunate that her parents were progressive thinkers and educators. They firmly believed in education for girls and ensured that their daughter was given the same opportunities as their two boys. She proved exceptionally intelligent and demonstrated a knack for mathematics and a passion for physics. Due to her academic excellence, she was offered entry to several prestigious universities, including the University of Michigan and the University of California at Berkeley.

When Wu arrived in Ann Arbor, she was shocked to discover that in 1936, female students attending the University of Michigan were not allowed to use the front entrance of many buildings unless escorted by a man. This overt sexism was troubling, so she headed to Berkeley.

When she visited the University of California at Berkeley, she was given a tour by Luke Chia-Liu Yuan, a physics student who would later become her future husband. Along with appreciating the cordial welcome, Wu was impressed by the faculty, which included Ernest Lawrence, inventor of the cyclotron, also located at UC Berkeley.

Professor Lawrence later described Wu as "the most talented experimental physicist he had ever known," and stated that "She would make any laboratory shine." Eventually, Wu came to work with the best physicists of the day, including Oppenheimer, whom Wu referred to as "Oppie." He called her "Jiejie," an affectionate term for "elder sister" in Chinese.

Of course, Oppenheimer, known as the "father of the atomic bomb," was a critical part of the Manhattan Project, as was Wu. However, she distanced herself from it when she realized the bomb's utter destructive force. In 1965, she advised Chiang Kai-Shek, the former president of Taiwan, who was then head of the Chinese Nationalist government in exile, never to build nuclear weapons.

In 1957, Dr. Wu had become famous for her experiments on beta decay. For six months, she tested a theory proposed by Dr. Tsung-Dao Lee and Dr. Chen Ning Yang. Their theory suggested that parity, which is the principle that says the laws of nature don't favor one direction over another, doesn't hold in certain nuclear reactions. However, they needed to prove their theory and asked Wu to help them. Dr. Wu spent six intensive weeks working day and night to test and confirm their theory; her research changed the way scientists understood the universe by disproving the old belief that parity was always conserved in weak subatomic interactions. Her research protocol will forever be known as the Wu Experiment. However, the two men went on to win the Nobel Prize for their theoretical work, while Wu's critical contribution was overlooked for many years. It is widely acknowledged that she was not awarded the Nobel Prize because she was a woman.

In the 123 years of the Nobel Prize in Physics, with a total of 226 laureates, there have been only five female winners. Dr Wu went on to win the National Academy of Sciences' Cyrus B. Comstock Award in Physics in 1964, the National Medal of Science in 1975, and the Wolf Prize in Physics in 1978, among other prestigious awards. In addition, Dr. Wu was the first female faculty member to teach at Princeton, and when she later joined the faculty of Columbia University, she became the first woman to hold a tenured faculty position in the physics department.

For more than forty years, Dr. Wu charted her own brilliant course in a field dominated by men and established herself by conducting authoritatively precise and accurate research to test fundamental theories of physics. She also became renowned for her steadfast promotion of teaching STEM subjects to all students, regardless of gender or any other characteristics subject to discrimination and bias.

In 2021, the US Postal Service honored Professor Emerita Chien-Shiung Wu with a commemorative Forever stamp.

Wu's husband was also a renowned physicist who completely supported her work and often cared for their son, Vincent, so that Wu could dedicate her time and energy to her lab. Vincent in his turn also became a physicist. And Dr. Wu's granddaughter, Jada Yuan, is a famous writer.

Flora Zaibun Majid—When Flora Met Spirulina

Spirulina (*Arthrospira platensis*) is a blue microalga widely known as a superfood. Even the esteemed United Nations has declared its value due to its sustainability, nutritional worth, and multiple health benefits. It is also one of the oldest food sources in the world, going back some three billion years.

When Flora Zaibun Majid met spirulina, she intuitively understood its value and relevance to Bangladesh, given its health benefits and economic potential. She tapped into her many years of scientific know-how to bring the promise of this blue-green alga to Bangladesh. Many people who met Dr. Majid described her as introspective and shy. Yet beneath that quiet veneer, she was a woman who overcame many obstacles to become one of the most respected and honored scientists in her country.

She contracted polio when she was only nine months old; the condition was misdiagnosed as typhoid, so for decades, she was given the wrong brace to wear for her handicap, which caused a lot of unnecessary pain. But despite this debilitating health issue, Flora excelled in her studies and was always at the top of her class.

She credited her oldest sister, Ruby, as a great source of inspiration for her excellent grades. "She would motivate us to study by promising us a box of chocolate." When Ruby married and moved away, Flora was heartbroken.

Despite the disappointment of her sister leaving, Majid thrived in school and entered Dhaka University, majoring in botany with minors in chemistry and zoology. Due to her academic excellence, she received a Fulbright Scholarship to do her PhD work at Michigan State University. But she almost didn't even make it to America, because while visiting her parents in Karachi, she fell from some rickety steps that collapsed, and she had to be hospitalized. She recalls that just before she fainted, she was worried that her father would be upset because she'd broken the stairs. Her father, however, was not upset at all, and she did make it to the states. However, her beloved sister Ruby died in a car accident. This tragedy almost derailed the completion of her PhD, but her parents and professors encouraged her to finish her degree in honor of her sister.

Upon her return to Bangladesh, Dr. Majid found work as a teacher, but was soon offered a position with the Bangladesh Council of Scientific and Industrial Research, and later went on to become the first woman to chair the organization.

Decades into her research, Dr. Majid was introduced to spirulina by an Italian entrepreneur who wanted to see if he could grow it on an industrial scale in Bangladesh. The climate and frequent monsoons there made it very challenging, and he gave up and left. However, she was fascinated with the potential of this blue-green alga and persisted with her experimentation. She finally discovered a way to grow this superfood that could be scaled up by using a growing medium different from those utilized in other places. Since her innovation, the spirulina

industry has vastly expanded in her country, bringing economic benefits
to Bangladesh and providing a nutritious supplement for millions.

To fully appreciate Dr. Majid's contribution, it is essential to note the
many amazing properties of spirulina:

- Fights malnutrition:
  Spirulina is rich in nutrients and minerals and is easy to digest.
  It can help with the absorption of nutrients even in a body that is
  significantly depleted.

- Improves child development:
  Fortifying complementary food with spirulina during the first two
  years of life can have long-term benefits for child development.

- Treats arsenicosis:
  Spirulina can be effective in treating arsenicosis, a condition that
  affects up to 3 percent of the population in Bangladesh.

- Environmental mitigation:
  Spirulina can be grown on a local scale to help mitigate
  environmental pollution.

- Livelihood development:
  Spirulina offers potential for positive economic growth
  in Bangladesh, particularly when grown locally for
  livelihood development.

- Protein source:
  Spirulina can be a protein source for fish and other farmed
  livestock as well as for human beings.

In a 2012 interview, Dr. Majid told a reporter, "By nature, I was always a
little bit scared of life because of my handicap. And because I was weak
in mathematics, I thought I might not succeed as a scientist, so whatever
success came, I was grateful for it. I didn't expect it. I kept my ambitions
small but possible."

A spirulina filament measures only about 0.3 millimeters, but she magnified this tiny micro-organism into a big industry with vast health benefits for her country. Flora Zaibun Majid is a shining example of how women can break barriers despite physical disability and life's many obstacles.

Mazlan binti Othman—the Astrophysicist with the Heart of a Poet

Mazlan binti Othman's first appreciation for the celestial came to her through William Yeats's poem "Aedh Wishes for the Cloths of Heaven," which she read as a child. Impressively, Mazlan recited the entire poem from memory during a video interview conducted in 2023.

> *Had I the heavens' embroidered cloths,*
> *Enwrought with golden and silver light,*
> *The blue and the dim and the dark cloths*
> *Of night and light and the half light,*
> *I would spread the cloths under your feet:*
> *But I, being poor, have only my dreams;*
> *I have spread my dreams under your feet;*
> *Tread softly because you tread on my dreams.*

> —William Butler Yeats, 1899

Mazlan binti Othman became an astrophysicist because it is a field that is scientific and yet unfathomably mysterious. She became Malaysia's first astrophysicist and has been a driving force in getting everyone in her country excited about space. With an aptitude for mathematics and solving complicated formulas, she was granted a scholarship to attend the University of Otago in Dunedin, New Zealand. She intended to study

physics, but after discovering astrophysics, she decided to specialize in
this unique discipline, which applies the laws of physics to astronomy.

When Dr. Othman returned to Malaysia, she started designing an
astrophysics curriculum for the national university. In 1990, she found
a powerful ally in Prime Minister Mahathir Mohamad, who asked
her to oversee the building of Planetarium Negara, the country's first
such project. The public, hitherto unacquainted with the mysterious
cosmos, was initially a little daunted by Othman's forward-looking
initiatives. But they quickly embraced the planetarium, which now
serves as a tourist attraction and a showcase of Malaysia's scientific and
technological innovations.

The United Nations got wind of Dr. Othman's work, and in 1999, UN
Secretary-General Kofi Annan asked her to become the director of the
UN Office of Outer Space Affairs (UNOOSA). This was too good to
pass up, so Dr. Othman headed to Vienna to take up the post. Although
"outer space affairs" sounds as if it might imply communications with
extraterrestrials, UNOOSA's purpose was to deal with issues of space
laws and international space cooperation between countries, monitor
space debris and collisions, and assess the risks of asteroids spinning
near Earth.

A couple of years into her UN post in Vienna, Prime Minister
Mahathir requested that Othman return to Malaysia to become the
Director General of Angkasa, the newly established National Space
Agency. As director, she was instrumental in launching Malaysia's first
microsatellite and its first astronaut, Sheikh Muszaphar Shukor, into
space. The project was executed in coordination with the Russian Soyuz-
TMA-11 space program.

In 2007, Othman returned to the United Nations for a second term as director of UNOOSA. Later, after retiring from the UN, she served on advisory committees and boards involving science and space, taught as a visiting professor, and became a senior fellow of the Academy of Sciences Malaysia. In 2017, she was named director of the International Science Council Regional Office for Asia and the Pacific.

Othman has been awarded the President's Medal by the Institute of Physics and the Polar Star Award by the Austrian Space Forum. She was also given the honorific title of *Datuk* by the government of Malaysia, which signifies respect and gratitude for her dedication. She is now retired but is still very active in promoting astrophysics. In 2023, she collaborated with an artist and a poet on a beautiful book entitled *Cosmic Connections Langkawi*.

Aditi Pant—First Indian Woman in Antarctica

Aditi Pant is a shining role model for girls; her life shows that they can reach for the stars or explore the mysterious depths of the ocean when they grow up. This maverick scientist, who became the first Indian woman to set foot in Antarctica, also has a long list of other accomplishments to her name.

She was born in 1942 in Nagpur, a city in central India. Her father was a diplomat who loved nature, trekking, and reading, and he was always curious about how things worked. At the dinner table, they would discuss a multitude of topics—anything from steam engines to the stars. Her mother, a medical doctor, taught her daughter how to cook from a young age. Every time they made dal or *sabji*, she insisted that her daughter measure each ingredient carefully for consistent results. Later, this made Aditi realize that one has to carefully measure everything in the laboratory to get perfect results.

She attended the University of Pune and obtained a bachelor's degree. She was inspired to become an oceanographer when she came across *The Open Seas* by Alister Hardy, a well-known British scientist and illustrator. The book's magnificent drawings of plankton, algae, and sea creatures mesmerized her, and she knew that her destiny was with the seas. However, to pursue her dream, she had to obtain an advanced credential in oceanography. Since money was a concern, she was overjoyed when the US government awarded her a scholarship to the University of Hawaii. There, she delved into marine sciences and immersed herself in the world of plankton communities and ocean ecosystems. Furthering her education, Aditi Pant completed her PhD in Physiology from Westfield College at the University of London.

When Aditi returned to India, she joined the National Institute of Oceanography in Goa. From 1973 to 1976, she dedicated herself to studying coastal regions and conducted extensive research along the western coast of India. She commented, "Very often, I was the only woman on the team. Local villagers, especially the women, sent their husbands or brothers to find out whether there was anything I wanted, including hot water for a bath in their own huts! This special treatment resulted in much leg-pulling by my colleagues about 'women' scientists, but secretly they were rather relieved that they never had to worry about me."

In 1983, she became the first Indian woman to participate in the third expedition to Antarctica as part of the Indian Antarctic Program. In extremely harsh Antarctic conditions, Dr. Aditi Pant conducted extensive research for four months, resulting in remarkable discoveries.

Her team also successfully built Dakshin Gangotri, the first Indian Scientific Research Base in Antarctica.

Dr. Aditi Pant participated in the fifth expedition to the Antarctic in 1985 as well, during which she carried out more research in oceanography and geology. For her outstanding contributions to the expedition, she was honored with the Antarctica Award. She is proof positive that women in any corner of the world can achieve their goals.

Dr. Esther Park—Selfless Pioneer for Women's Health

As a child, Dr. Esther Park, born Kim Jeom-dong, was a bright and intelligent girl. In 1886, when most girls in Korea were not given an education, she enrolled in Ewha School, the first modern educational institution for Korean women, which was founded by the American missionary Mary Scranton. Jeom-dong's father got her into the school because he firmly believed in literacy for girls.

She flourished in the exciting new academic environment, acquiring the Korean and Chinese languages, becoming acquainted with science and mathematics, and gaining a mastery of English very quickly. In 1894, her linguistic proficiency led to her becoming a translator for Dr. Rosetta Sherwood Hall, who had come to Korea on a medical service mission. This collaboration would set the course for Kim Jeom-dong's path to becoming a pioneer of women's health in Korea.

She wasn't particularly interested in medicine at first, but that changed when she witnessed an operation performed by Dr. Hall on a young girl with a harelip (a cleft lip). The girl recovered completely without any scarring and was saved by the surgery from a lifetime of pain and embarrassment. At that point, Kim Jeom-dong became fascinated with Western medicine. Dr. Hall took her under her wing, and even introduced her to a young man, Park Wu-San, who later became Kim's husband.

In 1893, they were married in the first Western-style wedding ceremony in Korea and then prepared to travel to the US, where Kim Jeom-dong would begin her medical studies. After their marriage, she officially changed her name to Esther Park. She was the youngest student to enroll in the Baltimore Medical College and obtained her medical degree with honors in 1896. Esther Park was the first Korean woman to earn a medical degree in the United States. But her joy was short-lived as her husband died from tuberculosis six months after her graduation.

Despite this heartache, she returned to Korea, making her the first female Western-trained medical doctor in her country. She began her medical missionary work, which combined her knowledge of modern medicine with spreading Christianity. She traveled to the most remote places to serve women and girls in need of medical care. During a cholera epidemic, she treated thousands of patients free of charge. Due to her selfless devotion, she neglected her own health and died from tuberculosis—the same disease that had taken the life of her husband— at age thirty-four.

In 2006, the government of Korea posthumously inducted Dr. Park into the Korea Science & Technology Hall of Fame. The Esther Park Award was established in 2008 by the alumnae committee of the Ewha School of Medicine to commemorate her achievements and award Ewha alumnae who carry on Dr. Park's legacy as women doctors and scientists.

Dr. Maggie Lim—Paving the Path for Planned Parenthood

Although Maggie Lim was born into one of Singapore's most elite and established families, she did not just sit back and luxuriate in wealth and high society. Instead, she worked tirelessly on behalf of unprivileged women and girls and was an activist who paved the way for a woman's right to choose.

Maggie was very smart. She skipped several grades and graduated from the equivalent of high school at twelve! She was encouraged to apply for the Queen's Scholarship but had to wait several years because candidates needed to be at least sixteen. Once old enough, she entered the previously all-male training program for the scholarship and won, becoming the only female winner in the scholarship's forty-five-year history. She then left for England to study medicine at the London School of Medicine for Women and the Royal Free Hospital.

When she returned to Singapore and started her medical practice, Dr. Lim was shocked time and time again by how so many women were drained by childbirth and poverty. Some of them even begged her to buy their newborn infant because they had no means of supporting another baby.

In addition, she also had to deal with the horrible medical consequences that women suffered from botched abortions. Because of her firsthand experiences, Dr. Lim became a strong advocate for birth control access, but it wasn't an easy path. She had to battle centuries of cultural orthodoxy that obliterated female individuality and sovereignty over their own bodies. The very ideas that women could take charge of their fertility and possibly even enjoy sex without procreation were seen as subversive and rebellious.

Dr. Lim and her staff had to withstand verbal assaults like, "Burn in hell for the wickedness of interfering with nature," and they were accused of "corrupting the young and scheming to depopulate the earth."

After Dr. Lim retired from her medical practice in Singapore, she entered a second phase of her career as a professor of epidemiology at the University of Hawaii and as the president of Hawaii Planned Parenthood. In 2014, she was posthumously inducted into Singapore's Hall of Fame.

> "My mother, Maggie Lim, was a woman ahead of her time,
> a trailblazer who understood that the well-being of any
> nation begins with the release of women from subjugation:
> the subjugation of ignorance, ill health, impoverishment, and
> the inability to regulate their own fertility. In this regard, the
> biggest gift my mother made to the world was that she
> was a forerunner of the women of generations to come."
>
> —Dr. Patricia Lim (daughter of Dr. Maggie Lim)

Maria Ylagan Orosa—Chemist, War Shero, and Inventor of Banana Ketchup

To fully comprehend and appreciate Maria Ylagan Orosa's deep dedication to her homeland and to fighting for its independence through food sovereignty, even at great risk to her life, we must begin with her childhood.

Maria was one of seven children born to Simplio Orosa and Juliana Ylagan in Luzon. As a child, she lived through the Philippine Revolution, a revolt against over 300 years of Spanish colonization. The Americans joined in the conflict and sided with the Filipinos to help them oust the Spaniards, setting events in motion that resulted in the Spanish-American War. However, when a peace treaty was finally signed, instead of gaining independence, the jurisdiction of the Philippines was transferred to the United States. Many Filipinos, including Maria's parents, were greatly upset by this betrayal. Her father, a steamboat captain, played a significant part in the resistance and transported supplies and soldiers on his boat in the battle for Filipino independence. War broke out between the Philippines and America between 1899 and 1902. After much bloodshed, especially on the side of the Philippines, a concession was reached and the insurrection ceased. Young Maria's exposure to the continuing struggle for Filipino identity and sovereignty shaped her sense of purpose.

Maria Orosa's natural curiosity and intelligence led her to study science. After a year at the University of the Philippines, she transferred to the University of Washington in 1916, where she attained degrees in pharmaceutical chemistry and food chemistry. She had to work several odd jobs to pay for her tuition, including spending summers in Alaska working at salmon canneries. There, she learned how to preserve and package foods on an industrial scale. This experience would serve her well.

In 1922, Orosa returned to the Philippines and joined the Bureau of Sciences. She was the right person at the right time in her country's evolution. Her goal was to ensure food security by supporting indigenous farmers and freeing Filipinos from dependence on imported foods that are far more expensive and culturally disconnected from the rich culinary abundance of their country. She experimented with preservation techniques like canning, dehydration, fermentation, and freezing using only locally sourced produce, including cassava, green bananas, and coconuts. Orosa created hundreds of recipes that have become pillars of Filipino cuisine, many of which were later co-opted by commercial food entities that never gave her credit.

The most famous Orosa recipe is the one for banana ketchup, which is a mixture of mashed saba bananas, brown sugar, vinegar, and spices. In an interview, Evelyn Garica, one of Orosa's living relatives, recalled, "She came up with banana ketchup. Of course, this is branded now, but it is her invention. It's a Filipino household must-have."

The Philippine government recognized Orosa's enormous contributions, and in 1927, the Legislature created the Division of Food Preservation and appointed her as its head. In this new role, she traveled widely to study different methods of food preservation and brought back techniques that would enable the world to enjoy the exotic fruits of the archipelago, including canned mangoes.

Then, in 1937, the Philippines again had to fight against foreign invaders; this time, it was the Japanese Imperial Army. America came to help the Filipinos, but Japan's invasion was successful, and they took many people as prisoners of war. Meanwhile, Orosa joined the resistance. Since food supplies were low, she devised ingenious ways to make nutrient-dense rations that could feed many people under siege. At great risk to her own safety, she smuggled preserved foods into Santo Tomas Internment Camp, where over 4,000 prisoners of war (mainly American soldiers) were held by the Japanese.

During the final battle for Manila on February 13, 1954, Orosa was wounded and taken to a hospital overflowing with the injured.

Tragically, the hospital came under American bombardment, and Maria died there, along with hundreds of others. She was fifty-one.

To this day, there are still Filipinos who remember how Maria Ylagan Orosa's dedication and food inventions kept their relatives alive decades ago. And banana ketchup has become a widely loved condiment in the Filipino diaspora.

CHAPTER FOUR

UNSTOPPABLE FORCE— BOLD ATHLETES AND DAREDEVILS

From the freezing ocean of Antarctica to the infinite frontiers of outer
space, Asian women have been there and done remarkable things that
have shattered stereotypes. They are showing the world that neither
cultural boundaries, gender bias, nor social restraints can limit true
courage and determination.

Kwon Ki-ok—Korea's First Aviatrix and Freedom Fighter

In 1917, Art Smith, the famous American pilot and aerial daredevil, flew
over Korea in his airplane, looping, darting, and weaving through the
clouds against the summer sky. His aerobatics drew wild applause from

the enormous crowd gathered on the ground, and standing amongst them was Kwon Ki-ok. She was a sixteen-year-old teenager who was so mesmerized by the spectacle of a man and his flying machine that she dreamed of having her own flying machine soaring through the infinite blue. That seemed like an outlandish and impossible dream at a time when women in Korea couldn't even vote and were still under the yoke of patriarchy, while the country was also under Japanese occupation.

Many Koreans were fiercely against the occupation, and Kwon Ki-ok was one of them. In 1919, she joined the March First Movement and the Korean Patriotic Women's Association as part of the resistance against the Japanese and was arrested twice. The second time, she was jailed for six months, and upon release, she had to leave Korea. She escaped on a rickety boat to Shanghai, where the Provisional Government of Korea was functioning in exile. Once there, she enrolled in college to learn Chinese and English and excelled at her studies to the point that she completed a four-year program in half the time. With her academic credentials in place, she was able to enter the Republic of China Airforce School in 1923. Even for many men, the aviation training was notoriously grueling, mentally and physically, but Kwon made it through and graduated in 1925. She had realized her dream of flying an airplane at the age of twenty-two. She was the only female pilot in her graduating class and Korea's first woman ever to fly an airplane.

She continued her aviation career with the Chinese Air Force, logging over 7,000 flying hours, and attained the rank of lieutenant colonel in 1940. In addition to her adventures in the sky, Kwon Ki-ok also fell in love and married while in China. Both she and her husband, Lee Sang-Jeong, served in the Provisional Government of Korea in exile, continuing their efforts to end Japan's subjugation of Korea.

When World War II ended in 1945, she returned to Korea, where she was instrumental in helping to establish the Republic of Korea Airforce. During the Korean War, she worked for the South Ministry of National Defense.

She received many recognitions for her service to her country, including the Order of Merit for the National Foundation. She died in 1988, having lived through some extremely tumultuous decades, not only for Korea but also on the world stage; yet Kwon Ki-ok had succeeded in realizing her impossible dream regardless of the challenges.

Junko Tabei—First Female to the Top of Everest and Beyond

"Within seconds, I could hardly breathe as an enormous pressure bore down on me. Confusion set in as I was tossed and turned upside down, the tent whipping around in somersaults amongst the churning ice. I thought for a moment I was dead," recalls Junko Tabei in her book *Honoring High Places*.

That chilling experience of an avalanche occurred thirty minutes after midnight on May 4, 1975. Thanks to the rapid actions taken by the sherpas guiding the team, everyone was pulled out from the heavy layers of debris mixed with snow and ice. There were injuries but no fatalities. Tabei fainted from being crushed underneath four of her teammates and suffered severe bruising as well as excruciating back and leg pain from being forcibly wrenched free.

But this near-death experience did not deter her. She and her team rested for two days after the avalanche and continued upward. Although she was still in great pain, Tabei maintained her position as team leader and led the ascent along with her sherpa, Ang Tsering. Twelve days later, at 12:30 p.m. on May 16, 1975, four-foot-nine-inches-tall Junko Tabei stood at the top of the world. She had become the first woman to reach the summit of Mount Everest.

When the news cascaded down the mountain, Tabei's name appeared everywhere, in print and across the airwaves. (She certainly would have gone mega-viral if social media had been around then.) The King of Nepal sent her his royal congratulations, and a parade was held in Kathmandu in her honor.

Of course, the Japanese government was ecstatic. They arranged for her to tour all over Japan, and there was a miniseries about the expedition. Sponsorship opportunities from big companies poured in, but Tabei declined them. "If I accept sponsorship, then climbing the mountain is not my own experience," she said; "It's like working for the company."

Junko was a frail child who discovered her passion for climbing at ten years old when she went on a school outing to climb Mount Nasu. Before long, she had summited all the major peaks in Japan and was ready for higher challenges. But before she could scale more mountains, she had to deal with the severe sexism of the time.

During the 1960s (and sometimes even now), women were expected to stay home while men went off to work. Some men refused to climb with Tabei, while others were convinced she was climbing in order to hook up with a husband. So in 1969, she formed the first all-ladies mountaineering club, aptly named the Joshi-Tohan (Women's Mountaineering) Club. Eventually, they organized a climb to Annapurna III and successfully made it to the top. Then, in 1975, after waiting several years for a permit, Tabei and her team headed back to Nepal for her epic climb.

The global adulation and attention never detracted Tabei from the core of who she was. She never bragged about her achievements and would simply say she was the thirty-sixth person to reach the top of Everest. After 1975, Tabei scaled sixty-nine other major mountains, and in 1992, she also became the first woman to climb the tallest mountains of the world's seven continents, known as the Seven Summits: Kilimanjaro, Tanzania, Africa (1980); Aconcagua, Argentina, South America (1987); Denali, North America (1988); Elbrus, Russia (1989); Mount Vinson, Antarctica (1991); and Puncak Jaya, New Guinea, Oceania (1992).

Junko Tabei is an amazing role model for female adventurers because she has shown that a woman can balance her quest for self-fulfillment and family life. She married a fellow mountaineer who wholeheartedly supported her, Masanobu Tabei, and they had a daughter and son. She even found time to pen seven books, which were all bestsellers in Japan.

Besides mountaineering, Junko Tabei was also committed to the environment. She was fully aware of the problem of waste in the Himalayas, from abandoned climbing equipment to plastic wrappers from food waste, and she actively contributed to the development of cleanup solutions. She was also the director of the Himalayan Adventure Trust of Japan, an organization working to preserve mountain environments around the world.

Junko Tabei was diagnosed with a brain tumor in 2012 but kept on climbing and doing motivational speeches and TV appearances. She passed away surrounded by her family at the age of seventy-seven.

*"Technique and ability alone do not get you to the
top; it is the willpower that is the most important.
This willpower you cannot buy with money or be
given by others... It rises from your heart."*

—Junko Tabei

Nor "Phoenix" Diana Kamarulzaman—
Hijab-Wearing Pro Wrestler

Meet Nor Diana, a petite five-foot-tall young woman who wears a hijab
while competing in the pro wrestling ring. She has become a role model
for other Muslim girls and women around the world. Wearing a black
and orange hijab and a costume with bright flames, her signature move
is jumping into the ring with arms spread wide open like the wings of
the mythical bird that rises from the ashes, in accord with her name as a
performer, "Phoenix."

Nor Diana became interested in pro wrestling when one of her brothers
introduced her to World Wrestling Entertainment (WWE) video games.
Her interest soon developed into a passion after she started watching
WWE competitions on TV, and she was inspired to become a wrestler
herself when she saw American female wrestling champion Mercedes
Kaestner-Varnado (who performs under the name Mercedes Moné,
after earlier using the ring name Sasha Banks).

In 2015 Nor Diana joined Malaysia Pro Wrestling and began training
with its founder, Ayez Shaukat-Fonseka Farid. Her four brothers all
supported her endeavors, and her father drove to many secondhand
stores to search for fabrics and decorations for her first wrestling

costume. Before long, Nor Diana quit her full-time job as a hospital technician and went to London to train at the Women's Pro Wrestling: EVE wrestling promotion company. She gained worldwide attention in 2019 when she beat four men to become the Malaysia Pro Wrestling WrestleCon champion.

Contrary to popular belief, pro wrestling is not a mere series of coordinated stunts. It requires intense training, agility, strength, timing, and the ability to focus while competing in a ring surrounded by energized spectators. It is performance art, wrestling, and storytelling all rolled into one. Outside of the ring, she is quiet and shy, but once she dons her costume, a different side of her emerges as she morphs into "Phoenix."

Pro wrestling in Malaysia is still a fledgling sport, although there is a growing fan base. Her dream is to be on WWE one day and match her skills against those of her idol, Mercedes Moné.

While many have cheered her on, she has also received a lot of backlash and hateful speech from conservatives who have criticized her for fighting in the ring with men and wearing tight clothing. But Nor Diana has learned to transform the negativity into fuel that energizes her desire to be the best.

In 2020, Nor Diana was recognized by *Forbes* "Thirty Under Thirty," which features young talents who are breaking barriers and making positive changes in the world. She was twenty years old when she received this recognition, and as the featured honoree, stated, "I want to inspire women not just in hijab but women in general. Nothing can stop us as long as we have passion and believe in ourselves."

Sunisa Lee—Unparalleled Gymnast and Role Model

From a young age, Sunisa was tumbling, somersaulting, and doing backflips in her house and backyard, so her father built a homemade balance beam for her out of a used mattress and other spare parts in his garage. It soon became evident to her parents that their little girl wasn't just hyperactive but had a natural gift for acrobatics. They enrolled her in a local gymnastics school, and Suni flourished.

She was a prodigy and progressed quickly in the USA Gymnastics' Women's Development Program, a ten-level system with progressively advanced skills and competition opportunities for each tier. She won the all-round state meet at just seven years old and jumped three levels the following year. At age eleven, she surpassed level ten and entered the elite program, making her eligible to represent the US in international competitions. She made it onto the Junior National Team at fourteen, and at eighteen, she brought home three medals from the Tokyo Olympics of 2018. She won a bronze on the uneven bars, helped the US team win the silver, and clinched the all-round gold medal. Lee became the first woman of Asian descent and the first Hmong American to win an Olympic all-around title in gymnastics. Everything was going splendidly after the Olympic Games until she woke up one morning with a swollen face, hands, ankles, and feet.

It soon became apparent that she couldn't go to practice and that something was terribly wrong. At first, the doctors thought it was a severe allergic reaction, but after a month of continued edema, Lee became really worried. Luckily, with the help of her sports doctor and several rounds of testing, it was uncovered that she had a rare kidney condition.

Mentally and emotionally, Suni Lee has had to deal with a lot in the past couple of years. Her beloved father fell off a ladder while trimming a tree and became paralyzed; following this terrible accident, she almost didn't make it to the Tokyo Olympics. She was faced with another tragedy when her aunt and uncle died from COVID in 2019. And then came her kidney problems, nearly ending her attempt to win medals at the Paris Olympics.

However, Lee stayed strong even though she was under a lot of pressure. As the months passed, the medication she was given for her kidney condition worked and she was able to train again. Amazingly, she qualified and made it to Paris for the 2024 Olympic Games, where she won a bronze for women's all-around, a bronze for uneven bars, and helped her team, which included Simone Biles, to overall gold for the US.

Beyond her spectacular wins and her financial success due to sponsorships, Suni Lee's rise to become a gymnastics superstar despite her health challenges has inspired countless girls, especially those from the Hmong diaspora; there are about 370,000 Hmong people living in the US. Suni's parents, Yeev (a health insurance manager) and John (a Navy and Army veteran) are of Hmong ancestry and immigrated to the United States from Laos. The Hmong, whose culture is ancient, are a people that have experienced terrible genocide and displacements for centuries. Like many immigrants who have had to leave their home countries due to war, they have often had a hard time assimilating to life in the US. So Lee's personal journey of triumph, made possible by her parents' sacrifices, has made a profoundly powerful impact and has brought pride and inspiration to her community.

Suni Lee's kidney ailment seems to have gone into remission. As of this writing, she is looking forward to either returning to Auburn University, where she is on a gymnastics scholarship, or perhaps heading to New York for the next phase of her awe-inspiring life.

Yuna Kim—Record-Breaking Stratospheric Skater

The defining performance of Yuna Kim's career began with a triple lutz-triple toe loop combination jump, followed shortly by a triple flip, and then ended with a double axel, all of which she executed perfectly while skating in the costume of a sexy Bond girl, as 007 theme songs accompanied her cutting-edge moves. For this dazzling short program, the judges gave her a total of 78.50, a score with which she broke her own world record by two points. The well-known Olympic sports reporter Philip Hersh described Yuna's performance as "stratospheric" and "transcendent." Then, she received another record-breaking 150.06-point score for her freestyle performance. With a total of 228 points, she won the gold medal and set a record combined score that would not be bested for seven years. She became the first Korean to win an Olympic gold in figure skating and the first female skater to surpass the 200-point mark under the International Skating Union Judging System.

Kim's parents lovingly supported her early on in skating despite being financially challenged. Her mom drove her to practice every day, and when her father's business wasn't doing well, they mortgaged their house so that Yuna could continue taking lessons. During Kim's early training, she had to duct tape her ice skates together because she couldn't afford new ones, and she also had to put up with skating rinks that were not on par with her skill level. However, her coaches told her she had the perfect physique and the talent to be a world-class skater, so she persevered. After training for a full day at the rink, she would continue doing exercises at home for hours. She was also able to learn new and challenging routines quickly.

At twelve, Kim won the South Korean Figure Skating Championships, the first of her many international successes. Highlights include the 2009 World Figure Skating Championships, where she became the first South Korean skater to win gold in the ladies' single event. At age twenty, her brilliant record-breaking performances at the 2010 Vancouver Olympics sealed her reputation as one of the greatest figure skaters in history. Sponsorships have made her one of the highest-paid athletes in Korea, even well into her retirement from skating.

Four years after Vancouver, controversy surrounded her final scores at the Sochi Olympics in Russia. The spectators were absolutely in awe of her magnetic and flawless performances. However, the Russian judges gave her a lower score than expected, and Yuna lost the gold to a young Russian skater. Allegations of corruption and favoritism circulated around the globe. The Korean Sports & Olympics Committee even filed an official complaint, but to no avail.

Yuna Kim calmly commented that she had already won gold and that there was more to life than skating. She is as elegant and gracious in life as she is on ice. After the 2014 Olympics, Kim announced her retirement from competition.

Since retirement, Yuna has become Korea's Olympic ambassador. She appears at many charitable events and is a UNICEF Goodwill Ambassador, children's rights activist, and the Ambassador for the Gangwon Youth Olympics in Korea. In 2022, she married singer Ko Woo-rim of the vocal fusion group Forestella.

Yuna Kim's stellar career includes winning gold at the 2010 Olympics, and silver in Sochi in 2014. She is also a six-time South Korean national championship winner (2003–2006; 2013–2014).

Yip Pin Xiu—Swimming for Gold, No Matter What

Yip Pin Xiu has refused to let physical disability keep her from making achievements as a Paralympian athlete: as of 2024, this competitive swimmer has six gold medals and two world records and is a four-time world champion. Looking at this astonishing list of wins, one would not think she has a severe handicap. She was born with Charcot-Marie-Tooth disease, a progressive degenerative condition that leads to uneven muscle loss, which can cause problems with the extremities, leading to mobility issues. The disease can also cause neurological and sensory difficulties. Yet Yip has turned her disability into a life filled with accomplishments, both in and out of the water.

She began swimming at age five to strengthen her body and fell in love with the ability to glide through water in defiance of gravity. At twelve, she started competing and has been winning competitions ever since because of her strong character and her determination not to let her disability become an obstacle.

Aside from her physical challenges, she has also had to deal with a lot of discrimination in school and from the public. People would stare at her on the street, and kids from her class would make fun of her while the teachers looked the other way. But instead of caving in, Yip Pin Xiu toughened up. At thirty-two years old, this disabled female athlete has accomplished much more than most people without any physical handicaps. She also became the youngest nominated

Member of Parliament in Singapore from 2018 to 2020. During her tenure, she advocated for issues such as inclusion in sports and tackled social problems that included campus sexual violence and workplace harassment against women. In 2022, Yip Pin Xiu was recognized for her outstanding accomplishments and was presented with the inaugural President's Award for Inspiring Achievement. She is also a member of the Singapore Safe Sports Commission and the National Youth Council.

Here is a recap of her triumphs, which are spectacular by any standard:

She is a five-time Paralympic champion in swimming (2008, 2012, 2016, 2020, and 2024) and the Paralympian world record holder for the 200 meter freestyle (2022), 100 meter, and fifty meter backstroke (2016) S2 classification. At the 2024 Paris Paralympic Games, Yip won two gold medals: one in the 100 meter S2 event and one in the fifty meter backstroke S2 event.

Yip Pin Xiu knows that her eyesight and muscles may be deteriorating, but she does not let this keep her from living life to the fullest. She once said, "There are many things in life that we cannot control; hence, we should not worry unnecessarily. We should focus on the good things we have in life. I am grateful for all I have in life, and I will continue to pursue and work hard towards my dreams and make an impact on society."

Naomi Osaka—"Like No One Ever Was"

Like no other tennis star before her, Naomi Osaka can boast of impressive and unique accomplishments both on the court and off. Her unique family background gave her an unusual start: her mother, Tamaki Osaka, is Japanese, and her father, Leonard Francois, is Haitian.

Her parents met while they were both college students on the island of Hokkaido in northern Japan. Although Tamaki's family expressed their racial prejudice against her relationship, the couple got married and had two beautiful girls, Mari and Naomi, in Japan. When Naomi was three, the family moved to Long Island, New York. Leonard started coaching his daughters in tennis when they were young, wanting them to become the next Venus and Serena Williams. Mari and Naomi became really good on the court, and both sisters turned pro.

Naomi Osaka quickly established herself, and at age nineteen, was selected as "Newcomer of the Year" by the Women's Tennis Association in 2016. In 2018, she defeated her childhood idol, Serena Williams, at the US Open. That win made Naomi Osaka the first Asian player to win a Grand Slam. In 2019, she won the Australian Open, lifting Osaka to the world's number one ranking, a first for any Asian player, male or female.

Many athletes who have become famous also become very careful of what they say and do in public because of concern about losing the money from endorsements and corporate sponsorships. However, Osaka is fearless in expressing her ethos by jumping into social justice activism or saying no when necessary. She withdrew from the 2020 Cincinnati Open to raise awareness of the shooting of Jacob Blake by police. That same year, during the US Open, Osaka wore masks that displayed the names of several African American victims of police brutality, including Breonna Taylor, Ahmaud Arbery, Trayvon Martin, and George Floyd, in a bold statement of her support for the Black Lives Matter movement. She also won the title in that tournament.

Then, in 2021, just before the French Open, she canceled a highly anticipated press conference, citing mental exhaustion. Her bold move caused a firestorm of controversy and sparked a global discussion on the mental health challenges endured by elite athletes who are always expected to perform at their best, no matter what. The press and the French Tennis Association were not amused and penalized her with a hefty fine. Osaka withdrew from the tournament. The four-time Grand Slam winner revealed on Instagram that she had suffered from bouts of depression since 2018 and that she would "take some time" away from competing.

Naomi Osaka broke boundaries and achieved spectacular wins both on the court and financially. In 2022, *Forbes* named her the highest-earning female athlete in history. When not playing on the court, Naomi pays it forward by working with various charities, including UNICEF and Play Academy. Notably, she and her family also started the Osaka Foundation in Haiti, which has built a twenty-acre training and living facility for young Haitian children focusing on tennis and education.

In July 2023, Naomi Osaka became the mother of baby Shai; her longtime boyfriend, rapper Cordae, is the father. Coming back after a hiatus of two years, Osaka is making her way back onto the court, and the world is waiting to see what she will accomplish next. After all, when asked what her career goal was, she smiled and replied, quoting from the Pokémon theme song, "To be the very best, like no one ever was."

Eileen "Ailing" Gu—Snow Princess, Supermodel, and Ace Student

Eileen Feng Gu (known in China as Gu Ailing) is a champion freeskier. (Freeskiing, a.k.a. "new school" skiing, is a hybrid type of alpine skiing that fuses freestyle skiing and snowboarding moves and involves terrain park features.) At the 2021 X Games, she won a gold medal and two silver medals as a seventeen-year-old rookie and then went on to wow the world by getting a gold and two silver medals at the Beijing Olympics.

It's not a stretch to say that Eileen Gu's life has a dreamlike stardust shimmer to it that is evocative of a grand fairy tale, except that the Snow Princess (as she is known in China) did not need a galloping prince riding in to help her achieve all that she has accomplished so far. Instead, the Olympian credits her mother and her maternal grandmother for her success so far in the many facets of her young life. Her father is American, but he is not a part of her life and seems not to have been since very early on. However, with her mother and grandmother's support, she graduated from high school a year early, as well as achieving a near-perfect score on the SAT exam before pursuing studies in quantum physics at Stanford University, an arc that is far from usual for star athletes (or really anyone). Versatile in her endeavors, she also works in modeling at a high level and plays piano, often preferring classical music. She may have come by her wide-ranging interests naturally from her mother. Yan Gu, Eileen's mother, came to the US from China to study biochemistry at age twenty-two and fell in love with skiing while attending university in New York. After earning an MBA at Stanford, she stayed in the Bay Area. Her daughter Eileen was born in San Francisco; Yan Gu started teaching her daughter to ski at age three.

Eileen's grandmother came to stay with them after retiring from her job as a senior engineer in Nanjing, China. Since she didn't speak English, she taught her granddaughter Mandarin; she told her Chinese stories and cooked delicious homemade Chinese food for her, which seasoned Eileen's gourmet palate.

Eileen Gu has admitted she has "a tumultuous love affair with fear." She is addicted to adrenaline and her athletic life on the edge, which spurs her on to compete and win big! Her three ski disciplines—superpipe, slopestyle, and big air—allow her to hone her technique and dazzle onlookers with gravity-defying tricks.

She often credits her grandmother, Feng Guozhen, for inspiring confidence in her; now eighty-five, she was an avid athlete in college and still enjoys jogging. On her Instagram account, Eileen Gu describes her as a "fiercely confident grandma who instilled in me my competitive nature." Eileen often states that her grandmother and her mother are two of the strongest women she knows. It is no wonder that Eileen Gu has such a strong bond with her maternal country of China. Her declaration that she would compete under the Chinese flag rather than that of the US caused quite a geopolitical ripple.

Growing up, Eileen traveled to China on yearly visits, and her fluency in Mandarin made her feel right at home. The main reason she has given for choosing to compete for China over her country of birth is that she feels she can make a powerful impact on inspiring girls in China to take up sports; in particular, she hopes some will jump into the world of freeskiing, which is still in its infancy there.

Off the slopes, Eileen is also the celebrity representative for over twenty-three brands in China and elsewhere. In 2023, *Forbes* estimated that she raked in over thirty million dollars from brand endorsements.

The Snow Princess supermodel is so beloved in China that her images are plastered everywhere, from billboards to newsstands and buses. Reaching such spectacular heights at only twenty years old could really mess with a girl's head, but what is notable about Eileen Gu is her sense of balance. She is that unique combination of boldness, brains, and beauty all wrapped into one.

Arunima Sinha—from Tragedy to Top of the World

Arumina Sinha's amazing ascent to the top of Everest is a testament to her mental toughness and unbreakable spirit. Accomplishing such a feat is tough enough for able-bodied adventurers, but Sinha is the first female amputee to reach the summit.

In 2011, she took a train ride on the Padmavat Express on her way to take an exam required for a position in the Central Industrial Security Force. She needed a job to support herself and her family, and she was hopeful that her reputation as a noted national volleyball player and her education in law would secure her the post.

But on that crowded train from Lucknow to Delhi, a gang of robbers entered the car that Sinha was in. The thieves targeted her because she was a female traveling alone. They surrounded her and tried to snatch a gold chain she was wearing, one which had been given to her by her mother. She put up a good fight thanks to her athletic abilities and was fending them off at first, but then she was simply outnumbered and overpowered. The compartment was full of people, but no one dared to come to her aid. Then, the unthinkable happened. The thugs grabbed Sinha and threw her out of the train. She endured horrible injuries due to being hit by multiple trains, ultimately resulting in her loss of one leg and injury to the other.

She was unable to move, and lay there floating in and out of excruciating consciousness; hours passed before anyone came to her aid. Once pulled from the tracks the next morning, she was left on the platform for hours until she was finally taken to the local hospital. Her left leg had to be amputated below the knee to prevent gangrene from setting in. However, the rural hospital was out of anesthesia, so Sinha was fully conscious when they sawed off her leg. The resident pharmacist donated his own blood to save her as there were no reserves.

Her right leg was also severely damaged, and a metal rod had to be inserted from her knee to her ankle. During the tormenting hours of her operation, news began to circulate about her situation, and she became a media sensation. Many people were shocked and outraged that a young woman traveling alone had been attacked on the train. Upon hearing the ghastly details of her rescue and amputation, the government got involved, and the sports minister arranged for her to be transported to the All Indian Institute of Medical Services in Delhi. Arunima Sinha and her family were relieved that she would at last be cared for at a top-notch hospital.

However, something unexpected happened while she was struggling to recover from the loss of her left leg and the overall physical trauma. When her story captured national attention, the sympathetic public demanded that someone be held accountable. No one could be found to take the blame, and accusations began to surface that the robbery had never really happened and that she had attempted suicide by jumping off the train. Someone even suggested that she'd had to jump off the train because she hadn't purchased a ticket and was trying to escape from the conductor. Of course, none of that was true, but it hurt Sinha's feelings to hear that such lies were being told.

As Sinha slowly began her rehabilitation with a prosthetic leg, she noticed that people were looking at her with pity, which annoyed her. She also could not dismiss the blight on her reputation caused by the baseless accusations of her injury being caused by suicidal self-harm.

One day, she read an article about Mount Everest and learned that no one had ever climbed the tallest mountain in the world with a prosthetic leg. With the help of a reporter, Sinha contacted Bachendri Pal, the first Indian woman ever to scale Mount Everest in 1984. Pal had become a mountaineering instructor and offered her full support when she learned about Arunima Sinha's goal of ascending Everest.

After receiving a grant from India's Tata Group, Sinha started training as soon as she left the hospital. She began a basic course offered by the Nehru Institute of Mountaineering in Uttarkashi, India. With determination and grit, she conditioned her badly broken body to climb the tallest mountain in the world. In 2013, just eighteen months after nearly dying, she was ready.

Her sherpa, Neema Kancha, almost decided to quit because he was convinced that Sinha was on a suicide mission as she doggedly pushed herself to keep on, even when she was bleeding and in excruciating pain. They finally reached Camp Four, meaning that only 3,500 feet remained for them to climb to reach the top. However, the area they needed to traverse was known as "the death zone" because of dangers from avalanches and sudden shifts in weather conditions, not to mention air so thin that many climbers simply are not able to carry on.

In an interview with *ABILITY Magazine*, Sinha said:

I saw dead bodies of mountaineers scattered all around. Some had turned into skeletons, and some were covered with sheets of snow. A Bangladeshi climber I had met earlier breathed his last right before me.

Ignoring the cold fear in the pit of my stomach, I trudged on. I told myself that [I could neither] go back from here nor [could] I die before reaching the summit. Our bodies behave according to how we

think. I firmly took stock of my fears and told my body that dying was
not an option.

At that point, her sherpa cheered her on, and she reached the summit, a
journey that in all took her fifty-two days. In 2015, she was awarded the
Padma Shri, the fourth-highest civilian award in India.

After her impossible feat, Arumina Sinha, with the help of sponsors,
founded a nonprofit school for disabled children, Freedom Fighter
Chandrasekhar Azad Sports Academy. She dreams of empowering
physically challenged people to achieve their dreams through sports and
to learn practical skills to make them an integral part of society.

Bhakti Sharma—Breaking Records Swimming in Antarctica

When Bhakti Sharma took a leap into the bone-chilling and literally
freezing waters of the Antarctic, she suddenly realized she wasn't
prepared for the situation! She had trained her mind and body to cope
with the extreme cold, but what she hadn't counted on was the density
of the water. In cold climates, water molecules contract together more
tightly, making it much harder to move through very cold water.
Therefore every stroke Sharma took in the freezing water felt twice as
difficult to execute, and she was really tempted to give up, return to the
boat from which she had jumped, and take a hot shower. Teetering on
the edge of that fateful moment, this is how Sharma described what
happened next. "So I lifted my arm and took a stroke. 'Now one more.'
So I took a second and a third stroke. By the fourth one, I saw a penguin
swimming underneath my stomach. It came up to my left and started

swimming with me. 'See? A penguin is cheering you on,' said that voice within."

Sharma took the penguin's appearance as a sign of destiny and persevered, stroke by stroke. 41.14 minutes later, she had set a world record for swimming the longest distance in the Antarctic Ocean. She is also the youngest swimmer and the only Asian woman to do so.

This aquatic feat of immense discipline and skill didn't happen overnight. As a child, Bhakti Sharma began swimming at only two and a half, coached by her mother, Leena Sharma, who took her to the local swimming pool and started teaching her to swim. Leena, an accomplished swimmer herself, wanted to share her love of being in the water with her daughter.

At just fourteen years of age, Bhakti Sharma braved her first open-water swim, in the Indian Ocean—a crossing of nearly ten miles from Uran Port to the Gateway of India monument in Mumbai. Three years later, in 2006, she powered through over fourteen hours of continuous swimming to cross the English Channel, and followed that up a month later by winning the prestigious Lake Zurich Swim in Switzerland. In 2008, she crossed the English Channel again, this time swimming with her mom—the only mother-daughter team to have completed the journey together.

Bhakti Sharma has said that one of the hardest parts of open-water swimming is not the physical challenge but feeling utterly alone in the vastness of the ocean. She notes that she has learned to face her demons and to treasure the hours of loneliness. She is now a world-famous motivational speaker who promotes girls' sports and programs in India. She is also in the process of completing a PhD in psychology and plans to teach mindfulness meditation in the future.

Samantha Tan—Racing for the Win and Equality

There's a biased notion that "All Asians are bad drivers." Well, Samantha Tan is out to prove otherwise both on the track and in the world. She is racing ahead to drive off stereotypes about Asian females and sexism in the media, proving the capability of women in motor racing along the way. Samantha is in a very competitive sport, and she's on the speedway to win, but beyond the racetrack, she is also competing to bring more equality and representation for Asian women in all fields.

Tan's father is a sportscar enthusiast, and Samantha has inherited his love for fast machines. When she was fourteen, she had the opportunity to ride in a Ferrari with a professional competitive driver. The exhilaration of the sheer speed and the feeling of the g-force as the driver shifted gears between lightning speed and intense braking to negotiate tight turns was absolutely thrilling for the young teenager. By the time they had finished the lap, she'd decided to become a race car driver. At age fifteen, she enrolled herself in racing school.

In 2014, at sixteen, her first competition was at the National Auto Sports Association, and she drove a 1991 Honda Civic. A special seat had to be made for her because she couldn't reach the pedals. That same year, she got behind the wheel of a Mini Cooper and came in fifth at the Canadian Touring Car Championship, as well as winning the Rookie of the Year Award. In 2017, she established her own race team, Samantha Tan Racing, and has been burning up the tracks driving a BMW M4GTB, going on to win back-to-back Pirelli World Championships in 2019 and 2020. Samantha Tan is also an outspoken force for gender and race equality. The world of motor racing is historically a conservative culture that is still dominated by the white, male, and wealthy.

Since Tan is a unique figure in motorsport, she feels pressure to be a good example and has had to build up her resilience and inner strength to change negative narratives that harm Asian women. With over 350,000 followers on Instagram, she has challenged herself to express what is in her heart. She did so eloquently in 2023, when in a very personal and empowering post, she revealed:

Being at the intersection of race and gender has given me the tremendous opportunity to define myself and success on my own terms. Today, I'm still learning and growing, but I'm no longer defined by the stereotypes that once held me back. I'm a proud Asian woman who knows that my experiences and my culture are valuable and worthy of celebration. I know that there will always be people who try to other me, but I am now able to stand firm in my identity and advocate for myself and others like me.

Samantha Tan's ultimate goal is no secret: to be the first Asian woman to win the world-famous race at Le Mans.

Kalpana Chawla—the First Indian Woman in Space

Kalpana Chawla was born in 1962 in Kamal, Punjab, India. Perhaps it was foresight that made her parents name her "Kalpana," meaning "idea" or "imagination," because while other girls her age liked playing with dolls, Kalpana preferred to draw airplanes and had an inquisitive mind.

After getting a bachelor's degree in aeronautical engineering from Punjab Engineering College, Chawla moved to the United States in 1982, where she earned a master's in aerospace engineering at the University of Texas at Arlington in two years. Undeterred by the Challenger space shuttle disaster in 1986, Chawla went on to earn a second master's and then a doctorate in aerospace engineering from the University of Colorado at Boulder in 1988. Later that year, she started work as a NASA scientist, researching power-lift computational fluid dynamics. In 1993, she joined Overset Methods, Inc., as a research scientist as well as vice president. She was also rated as a flight instructor and held commercial pilot licenses for airplanes, gliders, and seaplanes.

When she succeeded in being naturalized as a US citizen in 1991, Chawla applied for the NASA Astronaut Corps; she was accepted and began training in 1995, and was soon scheduled for her first space shuttle mission, joining the six-astronaut crew of the space shuttle Columbia. The two-week mission circled the Earth 252 times in late 1997, and she was in charge of deploying a Spartan satellite using a robot arm; Chawla had become the first Indian-born woman and the second Indian person ever to fly in space. After the mission, she did technical work for NASA relating to the space station. She was chosen for a second mission in 2000, but technical problems with the shuttle engine prevented it from going forward.

At last, she returned to space in 2003 aboard Columbia, but after a sixteen-day mission involving more than eighty experiments by the seven-astronaut crew, the shuttle, which had sustained heat shielding damage to a wing upon launch, did not survive reentry to Earth's atmosphere, and the entire crew was lost. Kalpana Chawla was posthumously awarded Congress' Space Medal of Honor, scholarships were established in her name, and an asteroid was named after her.

*"When you look at the stars and the galaxy,
you feel that you are not just from any particular
piece of land, but from the solar system."*

—Kalpana Chawla, at her first launch

So-yeon Yi—Against All Odds

In 2008, So-yeon Yi became South Korea's first astronaut and conducted experiments on the International Space Station on behalf of her country. She has become an icon of what is possible when a woman goes into aerospace science and thrives—in a field that is still dominated by men. Yi reached the stars against all odds.

She was born in 1978 in a small farming village near Gwanju, South Korea, where in that era, many women didn't attend school. Her grandmother, who grew up during the Japanese occupation, had been forbidden to learn how to read and write.

It was Yi's father who sparked her curiosity about how things worked. Her fondest childhood memories are of helping him fix things around the house, like mending the pipes and boilers. It was only when she got older that young So-yeon realized her Dad had to constantly tinker because they were too poor to buy new appliances.

She got really good grades and was able to enter the Gwanju Science High School, from which numbers of top colleges recruited. Sure enough, she got into the Korea Advanced Institute of Science and Technology (KAIST), which is the South Korean version of MIT. She graduated with a master's degree in mechanical engineering and later returned to earn a doctorate in biotech systems at KAIST in 2008. Decades later, she attended France's International Space University and earned an MBA at the University of California at Berkeley.

Although she was clearly intelligent and capable, she was in a field that was 99 percent male, and often she was the only woman in the room. At times, people would confuse her for a secretary instead of the researcher in charge of a project. Nevertheless, Yi applied for the Korean Astronaut Program, a mission to send the first Korean to space in collaboration with the Russian Soyuz space launch.

There were 36,000 applicants, ranging from doctors to teachers to firemen. In 2006, Yi was selected as one of two finalists. The other was Ko San, and he was slated to go on the mission with the two Russian cosmonauts. However, Ko was disqualified because he violated certain requirements. So, on April 8, 2008, So-yeon Yi stepped onto the Soyuz-TMA-12 and was launched into space. While at the International Space Station, she participated in experiments involving fruit flies, the effects of gravitational pull on facial muscles and on the heart, and the growth of plants in space. A fun food factoid is that South Korean scientists even created a special low-calorie, vitamin-rich version of kimchi for her. The spacecraft landed back on Earth eleven days later in Kazakhstan.

A few years after her stellar trip, So-yeon Yi left the Korean space program and came to the US. She is currently on the faculty of the International Space University, where she is training the next generation of aerospace adventurers.

CHAPTER FIVE

HER PEN WAS MIGHTIER— DAZZLING WRITERS AND POETS

Throughout history, the dark and oppressive weight of patriarchy has repeatedly denied girls and women the fundamental dignity of learning how to read and write. However, once given the opportunity to be educated, females of all ages have been putting pen to paper, fingers to typewriters, and lighting up laptops to express their unstoppable creativity and intelligence. Women wielding words have made the world brighter, more compassionate, and infinitely wiser.

Murasaki Shikibu—the World's First Novelist

The very first novelist in history was a woman from Japan who lived over 1,200 years ago during Japan's Heian period. She was a lady-in-waiting to the future empress, and in her spare time, she gracefully moved her ink brush across parchment by the light of a flickering candle, writing an enduring masterpiece that chronicled the daily lives of court nobles around her.

Murasaki Shikibu, known to the modern world as Lady Murasaki, was the world's first romance writer, social commentator, and gossip columnist all rolled into one. She is the famed author of *The Tale of Genji*, a timeless tale of desire, unrequited love, and court intrigue peppered with existential angst equal to any found in a modern-day romance novel or soap opera.

Even more astounding is that *The Tale of Genji* attracted immediate popularity and admiration from both her female and male contemporaries, and still continues to intrigue people today. In fact, in the many centuries since the book's debut, scores of academics have made their careers based upon their interpretation and analysis of this opus.

It is ironic that Murasaki penned such a detailed, intriguing, sensitive, and sensational account of her contemporaries, and yet we know so little of her own life. We don't even know her name: "Murasaki Shikibu" is essentially just an invented name used to refer to her in court records. During this time in Japan, it was considered improper for a noblewoman to have her own name. *Shikibu* is a rank that her father received through his work in the Bureau of Rites (i.e., ceremonies), and "Murasaki" is the name of one of the main characters in *The Tale of Genji*, a nickname bestowed upon the writer by a court poet during her lifetime.

Twelve centuries after Shikibu's death, Japan still honors her. All across the country, there are parks and monuments dedicated to her. Each year, a book prize in her name is given to the most promising female writer from Japan. In 2000, the Japanese government honored her by printing a 2,000 yen banknote with an image from *The Tale of Genji* and a portrait of Murasaki Shikibu. There is even a mini Murasaki-bot, a foot-tall robot that can recite her poems and fiction.

Ho Nansorhon—Brilliant Poet, Imprisoned Heart

Why would a woman born into a prominent and wealthy family, who was well-educated and described as being a beautiful and exceptionally talented poet, suffer from deep depression and die at the age of only twenty-seven? It is no secret that the combination of beauty and brains has not always been well received by male-dominated societies, whether from the distant past or in our more contemporary times. In Ho Nansorhon's case, she was a victim of strict Confucian orthodoxy, which dominated Korea's political and social life during the Choson dynasty of the sixteenth century.

She was born in 1563, and her father, Ho Yop, was a well-respected Confucian scholar noted for his code of honor. Her brothers were also scholars and distinguished politicians. It is said that she showed remarkable intelligence even as a child and gained recognition as a prodigy when she penned a very complicated long-form poem when she was only eight! It is also believed that she probably read all the books in her family's extensive library before she was forced into an arranged marriage at fifteen.

Being from an aristocratic and highly educated clan did not liberate her from the severe restrictions forced upon women during her time. In many ways, her high status made it worse, as it was deemed that women of noble families should function only as bearers of children to ensure the ongoing existence of the elite and ought to be kept at home to maintain their rarified existence. Ho Nansorhon and other women of her rank were therefore confined to the "inner" quarters, never to escape the dictates of Confucian doctrines, which demanded that women be subservient to men and be seen but never heard. Although her imagination was unfettered, she was physically and emotionally confined within her husband's household, from which he was often absent.

One can only imagine her suffering. To have experienced limitless worlds free of constrictions through her knowledge of books, tragically juxtaposed with her restricted life of being shut away in the women's quarters and neglected by her notoriously unfaithful husband, who was also jealous of her superior intelligence and artistry. Compounding her sorrows were the deaths of her two children: a girl who died shortly after birth and a son who died before reaching his second birthday.

It is widely rumored that she committed suicide. Before her death, she requested that all her poems be burned. She probably made such an affecting choice due to a sense of hopelessness and selfless consideration for her family's reputation. Due to the extreme gender bias of sixteenth-century Korea, it was considered improper for a woman to write poetry, and if anyone was to find out about these poems, the fact of their existence would damage the lineage of the family.

Fortunately for her legacy and for the world, not all her works were destroyed. One of her brothers, Ho Kyun, a prominent scholar and writer, saved some of the poems and then took it upon himself to make her work known to a wide audience. Ironically, she gained posthumous fame and honor in China, the home of Confucianism, before her work was recognized in Korea. Today, Ho Nansorhon is considered one of the finest poets of the Choson dynasty.

> *Cicadas sing mournfully—*
> *the wind*
> *desolate.*
>
> *The essence of lotus blooms*
> *decays*
> *under an icy moon.*
>
> *A beauty's hand*
> *holds gold*
> *scissors—*
> *sewing a coat for war,*
>
> *I raise the lamp's wick*
> *through the long night.*

Excerpt from *Deep Night Song* by Ho Nansorhon

Maxine Hong Kingston—Woman Warrior

In 1998, Maxine Hong Kingston experienced one of the worst things that could happen to a writer: her 165-page manuscript—and her home in the Oakland hills—went up in flames, and she had no other copy of what she had written. The charred book was entitled the *Fourth Book of Peace*. Although we will never be able to read the contents of that lost manuscript, the world has not been deprived of Kingston's remarkable body of work, a trove of literary gold.

Her magical-realism-inflected autobiography, *The Woman Warrior: Memoirs of a Girlhood Among Ghosts*, came out in the bicentennial year of 1976. It was perfect timing, because Kingston's story is an American story and a chronicle of rebellion. Her tale of a Chinese American girl coming of age in California won the National Book Critic's Circle Award and set off a wave of writing by women of color; suddenly, at thirty-six years old, Kingston became a literary shero. Her subsequent book, *China Men*, won another Circle Award in 1980. Her debut novel, 1989's *Tripmaster Monkey: His Fake Book*, thrilled both readers and critics.

Born in 1940 to Chinese immigrants who ran a gambling house in Stockton, California, Maxine got her first name from a very successful blonde patron of their establishment. When some shady fair-weather friends swindled the Hongs out of their gambling business, they then operated a laundry that employed the whole family, including Maxine and her five sisters and brothers. It was a life with a lot of drudgery, but Maxine was able to attend the University of California on the eleven scholarships she received. Although she originally intended to study engineering, she quickly switched to English literature. Upon graduation, she married a white man, Earl Kingston.

Throughout her childhood, Maxine Hong Kingston struggled with not seeing herself represented in the books she read. There were no stories of Chinese Americans in the Stockton library, and very few books featured girls. "In a way, it's not so terrible to be left out," she said years later in an *LA Times* interview, "because then you could see at a very early age that there's an entire mother lode of stories that belong to you and nobody else."

The girl in *The Woman Warrior* had her tongue snipped by her mother in accordance with the superstition that it would allow her to speak many languages. (In *Ami*, Audre Lorde relates having undergone the same frenum cutting.) Juxtaposed with the mundane school days and laundry work of Maxine's childhood in Stockton's Chinatown, *The Woman Warrior* illustrates the fantastic imaginings of a girl unfettered by chores and mere reality. Kingston cycles through the lives of her mother's female ancestors and speaks frankly of misogynistic traditional Chinese sayings, such as, "When fishing for treasures in the flood, be careful not to pull in girls!" and "There's no profit in raising girls. Better to raise geese than girls."

Perhaps then it is little wonder that Kingston has come under the strongest attacks from those within her own culture. Several Chinese men have gone after her, criticizing her for everything from taking creative license with Chinese legends to her marriage to a white man. Playwright and activist Frank Chin, on behalf of Chinese American male pride, has issued the most vicious and vitriolic assaults on Kingston's *The Woman Warrior*, derogating it as "kowtow" and "persona writing." Chin also lays siege to her persona as an example of "Ornamental Orientalia," calling her "a false goddess" created by "the worship of liars."

Clearly, Kingston struck a nerve with the power of her writing, touching on the critical issues of race and gender in a way that has caused *The Woman Warrior* to become "the book by a living author most widely taught in American universities and colleges," so noted by past US Poet Laureate Robert Hass. In Kingston's novel, her protagonist's inner battle rages silently within the confines of her mind—race, gender, spirit, and identity, straddling the duality of a culture that devalues girls while at the same time says "that we failed if we grew up to be but wives or enslaved people. We could be heroines, swordswomen."

A Warrior Woman's Literary Influence

Kingston credits Virginia Woolf as being a significant influence on her work. "Virginia Woolf broke through constraints of time, gender, and culture. Orlando can be a man. Orlando can be a woman." Inspired by Woolf to experiment with point of view along gender and race lines, Kingston has crossed over, she says, to where she "can now write as a man, I can write as a Black person, as a white person; I don't have to be restricted by time and physicality."

Amy Tan—Over Three Decades of Enchantment

Amy Tan's latest book is about birds she encountered in her backyard. It includes charming illustrations by the author. *The Backyard Bird Chronicles* (2024) is absolutely enchanting and has become another bestseller on the *New York Times* list.

This prolific writer is a supreme storyteller who has enchanted readers, both young and old, since her 1989 debut novel, *The Joy Luck Club*. The book's structure is laid out like a mahjong game, and parts of it were inspired by Amy's visit to China with her mother and meeting her two long-lost half-sisters. It was on the *New York Times* bestseller list for over forty weeks. In 1993, it was turned into a blockbuster film directed by Wayne Wang; it featured solely Asian actresses, which was a first in American cinema.

Through the years, Tan has consistently produced exceptional works, including *The Kitchen God's Wife, The Hundred Secret Senses*, and *The Bonesetter's Daughter*, the latter of which was made into an opera composed by Stewart Wallace, with the libretto penned by Amy Tan herself. And lucky children now have the opportunity to enhance their readings of *The Moon Lady* and *Sagwa: The Siamese Cat*, each of which has been made into an animated series for PBS.

Tan received the National Humanities Medal in 2021 and was inducted into the American Academy of Arts and Letters in 2022. She has also garnered the Carl Sandberg Literary Award and the Common Wealth Award of Distinguished Service. In 2021, *Unintended Memoir*, a documentary on Amy Tan's life, was released on PBS as part of the American Masters series.

Evelyn Lau—from Runaway to Luddite Poet

Evelyn ran away from home at fourteen because her parents objected to her goal of pursuing writing as a career. She did not just go and hide out at a girlfriend's house, however. For two years, Evelyn led a rootless life of homelessness that included couch surfing, drug use, prostitution, and liaisons with anarchists. She made a trip across the border from Canada to California, and even attempted suicide twice. But through all her travails, Evelyn always had pen and paper, and she kept on writing. After all, the reason she had run away was to protest her parents' restrictions. So, at eighteen, she proved her point by writing a memoir called *Runaway: Diary of a Street Kid*. It became an instant bestseller and was later adapted into a movie retitled *The Diary of Evelyn Lau* (1997), starring Sandra Oh. Decades later, her first book is still the publication that brings in the most royalties for Lau. Her poetry has won the Milton Acorn People's Poetry Award and the Pat Lowther Award for the best book of poetry by a Canadian woman. From 2011 to 2014, she served as the City of Vancouver's Poet Laureate.

Evelyn Lau says she takes refuge in reading and likes to disappear into books. She is also a Luddite who now focuses solely on poetry as her preferred means of expression. Avoiding Wi-Fi and cellphones, Lau spends her days writing poetry. Her latest book of poetry is *Pineapple Express*.

"Once you lived inside her body, / heard its thumps and gurgles, / that liquid house sloshing in the dark. // She hated the way you pressed your stomach / against the sink while washing dishes. / In the teenage bedroom you measured / your doughy thighs and pondered / where to cut. Hid Mars Bars in the dresser, / the desk, under the olive shag rug."

—Evelyn Lau

Ayu Utami—Powerful Words Against Repression and Patriarchy

Timing matters. Ayu Utami was a journalist in Indonesia during the reign of Suharto, whom many consider to be one of the most authoritarian, brutal, and corrupt dictators ever to rule in Asia. In the mid-1990s, many of Utami's friends were jailed and she was blacklisted. It was a very low point in her life, and since she couldn't work, the future was uncertain. She decided to turn to fiction as a way to continue her critique of the political repressions and corruption of the Indonesian hierarchy.

When *Saman* was written, Utami had no idea how it would be received. The book centers around four sexually liberated women and the life of

Saman, a former Catholic priest, and it is punctuated with supernatural and mystic encounters. The book could have been banned if the timing had been different because it was openly critical of Suharto's authoritarian regime and contained frank portrayals of female sexuality. Through her writing, Utami challenged a patriarchal culture that marginalized women and inspired other female writers in Indonesia to follow her lead.

But just eight days after *Saman* reached bookstores, Suharto was forced to resign. Overnight, a wave of optimism and the spirit of freedom ignited the country, and censorship was unofficially lifted. Ayu's book became an instant success, and everyone wanted to read it. Atami was awarded the Jakarta Arts Council Prize for *Saman* in 1998 and named a Prince Claus Laureate in 2000. She has published over fifteen works, including *Saman*'s sequel, *Larung*. Both titles are considered to be Indonesia's most influential fiction.

Since 2013, Utami has been organizing creative writing and analytical thinking courses at the Salihara Cultural Center in South Jakarta. She wants to help youngsters acquire the skills and understanding necessary to think critically and navigate the flood of information brought on by the internet and social media. Ayu is also exploring Javanese literary works in order to bring to light the Javanese concept of *rasa* (sensitivity), which has helped diverse communities in Indonesia live in peace with each other for centuries. Her upcoming work, a nonfiction book called *Anatomi Rasa* (The Anatomy of Sensitivity), is expected to be published in 2024.

Mieko Kawakami—a Most Feminine Feminist

Images of Mieko Kawakami resemble those of an actress or model. She certainly knows how to look good in front of the camera, often wearing deep red lipstick and fashionable attire. She is married to author Kazushige Abe, and they live in Tokyo with their young son. She was also a bar hostess, bookstore clerk, and J-pop singer before turning to writing as a profession. On the surface, there is nothing overtly feminist about Kawakami, but once you dive into the poetic and cerebral flow of her prose, it becomes apparent that she is one of the most lucid contemporary writers today. She creatively challenges the reader to contemplate issues of male entitlement, perceptions of the female body, and the social mores of our tech-obsessed society.

Mieko Kawakami has no formal training in writing, but her observations of daily life and thoughts on feminism resulted in a blog that garnered accolades.

She wrote her first novella, *My Ego, My Teeth, and the World*, in 2007; it won the Tsubouchi Shoyo Prize for Young Emerging Writers. Her other works include *All the Lovers in the Night*, which was shortlisted for the National Book Critics Circle Awards, and *Heaven*, which was shortlisted for the 2022 International Booker Prize. In 2022, *Breasts and Eggs* was translated from Japanese and published in over forty countries.

Mieko Kawakami, who started as a J-pop artist and feminist blogger, has more recently been sweeping the entire Japanese literary awards cycle: the Tsubouchi Shoyo Prize for Emerging Young Writers, the Murasaki Shikibu Prize for Literature, Granta's Best of Young British Novelists list, and the Akutagawa Prize, the most respected literary prize in Japan.

In a recent interview with *Bomb Magazine*, Kawakami stated succinctly:

It is often said that if a male writer writes about family, he is writing about philosophy or national history, but if a female writer writes about family, it is passed off as personal and trite. Those in power within the male-dominated literary world have never regarded women on the same level as themselves. Women writers are often praised for their work as being "effortless" and having an "innocent naïveté." These people believe that men write with sense and reason, while women write with their sensitivity. In their view, women exist only for their bodies, whether for sex or for childbirth, with no brains attached. In recent years, it has finally come to be recognized how sexist and invalid such perceptions are.

Well said! It is no wonder that Mieko Kawakami has become one of the most respected new writers focused on the feminine.

Celeste Ng—from Rejections to Bestsellers

The first piece of writing Celeste Ng submitted was rejected seventeen times, but she did not give up.

Since her first published short story, "Girls, at Play," appeared in the Bellevue Literary Review and received the Pushcart Prize in 2012, Ng has become a bestselling author who uses storytelling to immerse her readers in the most salient social discourses of our time.

Her first full-length novel, *Everything I Didn't Tell You*, is a murder mystery about the secret lives of the members of a Chinese American family living in Ohio in the 1970s. It received glowing reviews and was Amazon's Book of the Year, a *New York Times* Notable Book, and a winner of the Asian/Pacific American Award for Literature in Adult Fiction.

Her second novel, *Little Fires Everywhere*, is set in Shaker Heights, a well-planned progressive neighborhood in Cleveland; it challenges the reader to examine the nature of perceived order in society, art, and identity, and the energy demands and responsibility requirements of motherhood. It was adapted into a Hulu miniseries starring Reese Witherspoon and Kerry Washington, with Celeste Ng as a coproducer.

In her latest release, 2020's *Our Stolen Hearts*, she boldly confronts anti-Asian sentiments in a tale of a dystopian future where the "Preserving American Culture and Traditions Act" (or PACT, in the novel) dictates the rules of a racist American government that separates children from their dissident parents. Lucy Liu narrated the audio version of the book.

All of Ng's novels have made it to number one on the *New Yorker* Bestseller list; they have also been translated into multiple foreign languages and have been sold in over thirty countries.

After graduating from Harvard University and earning an MFA in writing from the University of Michigan, she was a teacher and editor before launching her full-time writing career. Celeste Ng's parents are immigrants from Hong Kong. Her mother taught chemistry at Cleveland State University, and her father was a physicist at NASA. She was born in Pittsburg, Pennsylvania, and moved to Shakers Heights, Ohio, with her parents and sister when she was around nine. The combination of her parents' migration and growing up in middle America has shaped Celeste's writing, and she considers herself to be a literary activist, tapping into themes of racism, identity, and the social constructs that both separate people and bring them together.

Marie Kondo—the Diva of Less Clutter and More Joy

Best known as the queen of decluttering, Marie Kondo has sold over ten million books and counting, which makes her a very successful author.

When then five-year-old Marie started tidying up her house and then tidying up after her siblings, she had no inkling that she would start a global decluttering movement and that her name would become a pop culture verb, as in "I'm going to Konmari my kitchen this weekend and get rid of all the junk."

Right from the get-go, Kondo had a gift and passion for organization. While other kids couldn't wait to get out of school at the end of the day, little Marie wanted to stay behind and tidy up the classroom. She has even shared that in her late teens, she learned that the National Library had an extensive collection of books on decluttering and organizing. However, one had to be of age to enter the library, so she joyfully spent her eighteenth birthday there.

In college, friends paid Kondo to declutter their rooms. She studied sociology and physiology and came to realize that tidying wasn't only about clearing a physical space; it also had a profound psychological effect that touched the soul. Her capstone thesis was entitled, "Tidying Up as Seen from the Perspective of Gender." She was also influenced by Shinto philosophy, which associates tidiness and simplicity with a sense of spiritual calm.

Soon after graduating from Tokyo Woman's Christian University, Kondo began working full-time helping people tidy up, and soon the waiting list for her services sometimes reached six months. Even though she was very busy, she wrote a book proposal for what would become her first book, *The Life-Changing Magic of Tidying Up*. A well-known Japanese publisher won the bid for her book, and she cranked it out in a few months with the help of an editor. That was in 2010; since that time, her books have been translated into forty-four languages and have sold millions of copies worldwide.

In 2015, she was seen by umpteen Netflix viewers in *Tidying Up with Marie Kondo*, becoming in the process a decluttering guru to even more messy people. And in 2021, the streaming platform brought her back in *Sparking Joy with Marie Kondo*, in which she shared her life-changing tidying methods with three businesses and their employees. She is known to have said, "I'd like to tidy up the entire planet. I would go anywhere if there were something that needs tidying."

The "spark joy" method involves assessing your emotional attachment to objects, expressing gratitude for what you have, and letting go of what no longer helps you. According to Kondo, sorting one's belongings into categories and then choosing to keep only what "sparks joy" teaches us how to respect what we have and how to be more in harmony with our living spaces.

Min Jin Lee—Meticulous Storyteller

Min Jin Lee was seven when she and her family immigrated to America. Her father, who had experienced the trauma of the Korean War, wanted to keep his children and wife safe from future conflicts.

In young Min Jin's mind, the thought of coming to America conjured up scenes from Cinderella, and the future author noted that she was quite disappointed when she arrived at JFK Airport in 1976. The family settled in Queens, but there were no magical princes or princesses decked out in royal finery riding in bejeweled coaches or castles made of candy canes, just lots of people with serious faces hurrying here and there and drably colorless buildings. Min Jin did eventually find magic—in the endless shelves of books at the public library. She sees libraries as miraculous places where a young girl (or anyone) can enter into endlessly different worlds.

Lee's love of books was nourished by being able to visit the library, and this is what prompted her desire to become a writer. However, she first studied history at Yale, and then law at Georgetown, and went on to become a corporate lawyer for a couple of years. The long hours required in that profession, together with a bout of major illness, caused her to examine her life, and she eventually answered the call of the muse and began to seriously write.

Her first novel, *Free Food for Millionaires*, tells the story of a young Korean American woman determined to carve out a place for herself in New York high society. *The Times* of London named it as one of its Top Ten Novels of the Year, and it was also a *New York Times* Editor's Choice. It would take Min Jin Lee another ten years to write her next novel, *Pachinko*. It is an epic work of historical fiction that spans four generations of a Korean family in Japan and underlines the discrimination they faced from Japanese society. *Pachinko* was made into a television series, premiering on Apple TV on March 25, 2022. It received critical acclaim, particularly for its cinematography, writing, and cast performances.

Min Jin Lee writes long novels with evident passion, meticulous research, and extraordinary narrative. She is also an outspoken advocate against discrimination and is proud to use her voice and visibility to support Asian Americans against anti-Asian hate.

Christina Vo—Writing Memoirs That Heal

Christina Vo has had an eclectic career, starting in international development and communications with roles at UNICEF in Hanoi, the World Economic Forum in Geneva, and at other nonprofits. Currently, she works as an associate director of donor relations for Stanford University's medical center development team. In her twenties, she moved to Vietnam, which helped her to reconnect with her heritage and find a sense of belonging that she hadn't felt growing up in the US, an experience that helped inspire her to use writing as a powerful tool for self-reflection and healing. Her first book, a memoir, became an element of her healing process.

Christina Vo was born in 1983 to parents who immigrated from Vietnam. Her father is a retired physician and an independent researcher of Vietnamese history and culture as well. Christina's mother passed away from cancer when she was fourteen. That loss caused a fundamental void and made Christina Vo question her life in ways that eventually inspired her to write her first memoir, *The Veil Between Two Worlds: A Memoir of Silence, Loss, and Finding Home*. It delves into themes such as loss, intergenerational trauma, healing, identity, and the concepts of home and reconciliation. This first published work emerged from her deep personal journey of dealing with sorrow and healing. After having lost her mother at such a young age, she spent much of her life searching for a connection to her cultural roots. *The Veil Between Two Worlds* reflects on the ways grief shaped her and how she navigated life, spirituality, and identity.

After the loss of her mother, Christina's father grew distant, and she felt a need to cross the silent divide. For this reason, her second memoir, *My Vietnam, Your Vietnam*, is a dual memoir in which the chapters alternate between the perspectives of the daughter and father. It was inspired by her desire to understand the complexities of her relationship with her father and their shared connection to Vietnam. She wanted to explore the generational trauma of the Vietnam War and how her father's experiences had shaped both their lives, even though they each experienced "Vietnam" very differently.

One illuminating aspect of her life has been the process of reconciling with her grief and transforming it into a source of growth.

Hoa Nguyen—the Soul of a Poet

Hoa Nguyen was born in the Mekong Delta of Vietnam and came to the United States as a child. From a young age, she desired to be a poet; she recalls that in sixth grade, she chanced upon an anthology of Vietnamese poetry translated into English. The opening line of the introduction said, "The Vietnamese people have always believed that they are poets." Reading that sentence inspired her to follow her passion.

However, on the path to realizing her dream of becoming a poet, Nguyen had to work in some other fields: she was a waitress, a business writer for a consulting firm, a tour guide, and an administrator for a university. In addition, she also taught creative writing and cofounded and ran a small poetry press called *Skanky Possum Publications* for a few years with her husband, Dale Smith.

Through it all, Nguyen continued composing poems, and she has published several books of poetry, including *Red Juice: Poems 1998–2008, Violet Ingots,* and *A Thousand Times You Lose Your Treasure,* which won the Canada Book Award and was a finalist for a National Book Award in 2021. Currently, Nguyen teaches poetry and creative writing at Toronto Metropolitan University.

In a submission to the fiftieth anniversary issue of *The Capilani Review*, Nguyen beautifully describes the essence of poems: "I call upon a poem as a gathering of language that includes the poet and poetry, that includes the dead, that includes readers present and imagined. Occasions for language that can accept the unknowable, poems trace distance."

Jhumpa Lahiri—Virtuoso Writer in Two Languages

In the history of the Pulitzer Prize, there have only been a few debut authors who have been awarded the coveted medal, and Jhumpa Lahiri, born Nilanjana Sudeshna Lahiri, is on that enviable list. Her collection of short stories, *Interpreter of Maladies*, came out in 1999 and won the Pulitzer in 2000. It has been translated into many languages and has sold over fifteen million copies. The book also captured the PEN/ Hemingway Award for best debut fiction. Lahiri was named one of the "Twenty Writers for the Twenty-First Century" by the *New Yorker*, which published three stories from *Interpreter of Maladies* in its pages prior to the book's publication. These are enormous accomplishments for an author who once described her groundbreaking book as just "nine little stories." They are evocative tales of the Indian diaspora, exploring themes including the immigrant experience, cultural differences, love, family, and identity.

Since her debut book, Lahiri has continued to enrich the world of literature with her first novel, *The Namesake*, which was an instant bestseller and was adapted into a movie of the same name directed by Mira Nair. This was followed by a second collection of short stories entitled *Unaccustomed Earth* and another novel, *The Lowland*, which was shortlisted for the Booker Prize in 2013.

At that point, after Lahiri's phenomenal success, she gave up English for years, reading and writing almost exclusively in Italian. Very few authors write in a language they learn as adults, but Lahiri decided to use Italian to express the current flow of her artistry. In 2014, she wrote her first book in Italian entitled *In Altre Parole*, or *In Other Words* in English. Her latest work, *Roman Stories*, was written in Italian and translated into English by Lahiri and Todd Portnowitz.

Arundhati Roy—Fearless and Unflinching Dissident

From the start, Arundhati Roy was slated to have an extraordinary life. She was born in 1960 in Bengal; her father was a Hindu tea planter, and her mother was a Christian teacher and social activist who founded a school called Corpus Christi in Aymanam, India. Arundhati received her early education at her mother's school and was encouraged to be a freethinker and develop independence. She skillfully demonstrated her independence by leaving home at sixteen and surviving on her own for seven years, making money by selling empty beer bottles while living in a small hut with a tin roof. While managing to live on her own at such an early age, she made astute observations of how Islam, Hinduism, and Christianity shaped life in India and the social dynamics that resulted from colonization.

Although she went on to study in Delhi to be an architect, Roy dreamed of being a writer. She wanted to express her observations and thoughts with words on paper rather than designing houses. After a series of odd jobs and a marriage that ended in divorce, she wrote and costarred in the film *In Which Annie Gives It Those Ones* (1989) and later wrote the script for *Electric Moon* (1992) and several television dramas.

After acting and writing for television, Roy creatively fictionalized her life experiences and keen observations into her first novel, *The God of Small Things*, which won the prestigious Booker Prize. She was the first woman of Indian heritage to receive that honor. The book was translated into forty languages and sold over six million copies. In 2019, it was named one of the BBC's "100 Novels That Shaped Our World." Twenty years would pass before Roy wrote another novel, *The Ministry of Utmost Happiness*, which enchants the reader with tales of eccentric characters living through some of the darkest moments in India's modern history.

Arundhati Roy is not only one of the most accomplished writers of our time, she is also a fearless activist and feminist who has not been afraid to voice her opinion on political and social situations in India and worldwide. The reason there was such a long gap between her two novels is because Roy decided to focus on nonfiction works, including *The Cost of Living*, which criticized the Indian government for building the Narmada Valley dam, which forced the displacement of many people and flooded over 100 villages. Her other political and social writings include *The Algebra of Infinite Justice*, a collection of essays on social and environmental issues, and *The Ordinary Person's Guide to Empire*.

In 2003, she was awarded the Lannan Prize for Cultural Freedom in recognition of her courageous work promoting social justice. She has since published a further collection of essays examining the dark side of democracy in contemporary India, *Listening to Grasshoppers: Field Notes on Democracy*. Arundhati Roy's long-awaited memoir, *Mother Mary Comes to Me*, will be published on September 4, 2025.

CHAPTER SIX

BRILLIANCE UNBOUND— VIRTUOSO WOMEN IN THE ARTS

The life of a professional artist can be perilous, especially if you are a woman. Through the centuries, only a few female artists have been recognized as on par with their male counterparts. If a woman decides to venture into experimental art, she may be considered mad or "hormonal," but when a man does the same, he is looked upon as being an eccentric visionary and becomes the darling of the avant-garde. For Asian women, the path can be even more challenging. Many Asian parents want their children to be doctors, lawyers, computer programmers, or engineers; anything but the seeming frivolity of being an artist! Culturally, Asian women are expected to prioritize family over personal ambitions, and becoming an artist can be looked upon as being indulgent or self-centered. And yet, the longing to communicate the hidden landscapes within our souls through the creative process is undeniable. From a Ming Dynasty illustrator who defied sexist restrictions on her art to become famous and financially successful—despite bound feet—to a groundbreaking ninety-five-year-old multimedia conceptual artist who stuns with her success, awesome Asian women artists are flourishing.

Using the Canvas to Change the World

Wen Shu—Ming Dynasty Maestro of Brush and Ink

Wen Shu, a rare female illustrator and painter in sixteenth-century China, lived during the Ming Dynasty, when Neo-Confucianism was the order of the day and foot-binding was at its most restrictive. Since she was from an elite family, her feet were bound.

Her great-grandfather and father were well-known landscape painters. Her father trained Wen Shu in painting, although women were limited to drawing flowers and insects. Images of landscapes or figures were considered too masculine and grand for females to accomplish. Despite the restrictions on her creativity and artistry, Wen excelled. She rendered every blade of grass, every flower petal, and every insect wing with such detailed beauty and unique style that her works were highly sought after. She also became an art tutor to other women.

It is important to note that in addition to being confined by the suffocating restrictions placed on Chinese women in sixteenth-century China, she was also crippled by the cruel practice of foot-binding, which was designed to keep women physically handicapped and reliant on male protection and financial support.

The ironic situation for Wen Shu is that although she married into a well-established family and her husband was a painter and scholar, he was neither interested in nor capable of making the amount of money needed to sustain their life of nobility, let alone support their children. She not only performed her womanly duties within a Confucian household but also kept the family financially afloat.

Wen Shu died at the age of thirty-nine. Although she lived over 400 years ago, her ink-on-paper artworks reveal her magnificent artistry, which overcame patriarchal limitations.

Ruth Asawa—Weaving Activism and Hope

Ruth Asawa was born during the Great Depression, and her parents were Japanese immigrants who eked out a meager living as farmers in Southern California. On a February evening in 1942, FBI agents barged into their home and arrested her father, and he was taken away to an internment camp in New Mexico. Ruth, her mother, and her siblings were taken to the Santa Anita Racetrack, which had been turned into a makeshift detention center. They were forced to live in horse stalls that always had the terrible aroma of horse dung.

During her incarceration in California, Ruth learned perspective drawing from fellow prisoners who had been illustrators for Disney Studios. She took to drawing immediately, finding it a means of expressing herself as well as a way to survive the harsh conditions of internment. Later, Ruth and her family were relocated to another internment camp in Arkansas, where they eventually reunited with her father. At the Rohwer Relocation Center, Ruth spent every hour of her free time drawing; she graduated from high school while confined there.

After leaving the internment camp, Ruth attended Black Mountain College, an avant-garde experiential art school in North Carolina. Her time there profoundly influenced her art and her philosophy, as well as her personal life when Ruth met Albert Lanier, a fellow student. The couple married in 1959, against the wishes of their respective parents. After their wedding, they moved to San Francisco because it was a city that was relatively more supportive of interracial marriages.

Ruth raised their kids during the day and worked in her art studio at night. Over time, she developed a distinctive style that set her apart as one of the most accomplished sculptors and illustrators in the modern era. Asawa is best known for her woven masterpieces made from wire—playful and complex biomorphic sculptures that are at once substantial and diaphanous.

When asked about her creative process, she said: "My curiosity was aroused by the idea of giving structural form to the images in my drawings. These forms come from observing plants, the spiral shell of a snail, seeing light through insect wings, watching spiders repair their webs in the early morning, and seeing the sun through the droplets of water suspended from the tips of pine needles while watering my garden."

Throughout her life, she created beautiful and stellar masterpieces, including illustrations, woven art, and art installations; activism was also an integral part of her artistic journey. Ruth was passionate about making art accessible to all children. In 1968, she and a fellow parent, architectural historian Sally Woodridge, opened the Alvarado School Art Workshop on a shoestring. They had no funding and used milk cartons, bits of yarn, and baker's clay as the raw materials to teach kids of all income levels. Asawa and Woodbridge were visionaries who understood the power of the visual and performing arts to positively influence a child's life, transforming their future. A few years later, Ruth became a member of the San Francisco Arts Commission and began lobbying politicians and charitable foundations to support arts programs that would benefit young children. Her tireless dedication led to the founding of a public arts high school in San Francisco in 1982; in 2010, it was renamed the Ruth Asawa San Francisco School of the Arts in her honor.

The Alvarado School Art Workshop has evolved into the San Francisco Arts Education Project (SFArtsED), and so far, it has offered more than 300,000 elementary and middle school students an opportunity to dance, paint, sing, act, weave, draw, drum, stitch, and sculpt—all mentored by working artists. Ruth Asawa is a recipient of the National Medal of Arts, the US government's highest award given to artists and patrons of the arts. In 2020, the US Postal Service honored her work by producing ten stamps commemorating her well-known wire sculptures.

Yoko Ono—Avant Savant

One of the most controversial figures in rock history, Yoko Ono was an acquired taste for most of those willing to go with her past the edge of musical experimentalism. Unfairly maligned as the woman who broke up the Beatles, she is a classically-trained musician and was one of New York's most cutting-edge artists before the Fab Four even cut a record. Born in Tokyo in 1933, she moved to New York in 1953 and attended Sarah Lawrence, but even then had trouble finding an artistic form where she fit; her poetry was criticized for being too long, her short stories too short. Then she was befriended by avant-garde composers like Arnold Schoenberg and John Cage.

Soon, Yoko Ono's originality was making a splash in post-beatnik Greenwich Village, going places even Andy Warhol hadn't dared with her art films of 365 nude derrieres, her performance art (including inviting people to cut her clothes off her), and her bizarre collages and constructions. Called the "High Priestess of the Happening," she enthralled visitors to her loft with such art installations as tossing dried peas at the audience while whirling her long hair. Ono had an ability to shock, endless imagination, and a talent for attracting publicity that P.T. Barnum himself would've envied!

When John Lennon climbed the ladder on that fateful day to peer at the artful affirmation she created in her piece "Yes," rock'n'roll history was made. Their collaborations—The Plastic Ono Band, Bed-Ins, Love-Ins, Peace-Ins, and their son Sean Lennon—have created a vibrant legacy, one that continues to fascinate a world that has finally grudgingly accepted and respected this bona fide original. Yoko Ono's singing style—howling and shrieking in a dissonant barrage—was a major influence on the B-52s, as well as a generation of riot grrl punk rock bands.

Now Yoko Ono and her talented son Sean tour together and work on behalf of causes to which they are committed—the environment, peace, and Tibet. Ono, whose sweet speaking voice belies the steely strength underneath that has enabled her to endure for so long, explains her sheroic journey in the preface she contributed to Gillian G. Gaar's excellent book on women in music, *She's a Rebel*. In it, she relates her pain at how her father discouraged her dream of becoming a composer, doubting her "aptitude" because of her gender. " 'Women may not be good creators of music, but they're good at interpreting music' was what he said." Noting with pleasure that times have changed, she points to the valiant efforts made by "women artists who kept making music despite overwhelming odds till finally the music industry had to realize that women were there to stay."

In hindsight, Yoko Ono was breaking real musical ground at a time when others were cranking out bubble gum pop and imitating—who else—the Beatles. Her feminism gets lost in the shuffle of the attention to her as an iconoclast. She played an enormous part in awakening John Lennon's interest in the women's movement, and they attended an international feminist conference together in 1973 as well as collaborating on writing songs inspired by the women's movement, including "Woman is the N****r of the World." Much of her musical output in the seventies was on the theme of feminism; her song "Sisters O Sisters," a reggae rhythm number, is one of her finest works. Yoko Ono's sheroism lies in her intense idealism and her commitment to making this a better world.

"Art is like breathing for me. If I don't do it, I start to choke."

—Yoko Ono in 1973

Na Hye-seok—Radical Feminist Ahead of Her Time

"I'm a woman, and I am a Korean woman—a woman shackled by Korean society's family conventions. If a woman tries to stand on her own, she will feel pressure from all quarters, and if she aspires to accomplish something, she will be criticized from all sides."

—Na Hye-seok, "Kyong Hui"

In myriad ways, Na Hye-seok was a woman born far ahead of her time. This may still be true even at our current moment, since the core purpose of her art is the total liberation of all social-norm-driven restrictions and expectations on women while also allowing each woman to fully express her sexuality and creativity. That's a tall order even today, and it was definitely the case during the era in which Na Hye-seok lived.

Born into a wealthy Korean family in 1896, she became the country's first professional woman painter, producing some of the earliest Western-style paintings in Korea. She also wrote and published feminist novels and short stories. True to her essence, she did not confine herself to one artistic medium. In addition to painting, Na Hye-seok wrote fiction, poems, travelogues, and critical essays. She boldly criticized patriarchy and advocated for women's liberation, including equality in sexual expression, and felt that women should be free to pursue relationships outside of marriage.

In 1918, while studying in Japan, at age twenty-two, Na Hye-seok wrote what is considered to be the first feminist short story in Korean literature, "Kyong Hui." It is a semi-autobiographical account of a woman returning home from studying abroad, where she is confronted by her own family and neighbors, who express skepticism as to the value of educating girls. Through this novel, she voiced her frustration with the strict gender roles ingrained in the patriarchal culture of Korea.

In March of 1919, Na joined the massive uprising of Koreans against the colonial rule of Japan. She was arrested and jailed for six months, but thanks to her family's influence and their financial ability to hire a good lawyer for her, she was eventually released. The following year, she married Kim Woo-young, the lawyer who had defended her and helped her get out of jail. At the beginning of their marriage, he was very supportive of her art and activism. They had an unconventional and extremely progressive relationship in which he allowed her to pursue her art.

In 1921, Na held an exhibition of her paintings that attracted over 5,000 attendees, the first time a female artist ever had a solo art exhibit in Korea. It received rave reviews, and she sold many paintings. Along with her success as a painter, Na Hye-seok also cofounded a feminist magazine, *Sinyoja* (*New Woman*).

After Na gave birth to her first child, her husband was given a post in Manchuria, and they moved there. She produced many paintings during this time. In 1927, her husband was offered the chance to embark on an extended tour of Europe, so they left their three children in the care of family members and traveled to Paris. On this trip, she had an affair with a well-known Korean political figure named Choi Rin, a decision that would mark a dramatic shift in her life.

When her husband learned about the affair, he publicly shamed her and filed for divorce. Na was both stunned and furious at the double standard since it was known that her husband had mistresses. After her husband filed for divorce, he also cut off her ability to see her children. In a fit of anguish, Na sued her former lover, Choi Rin, accusing him of seducing and abandoning her. Although she didn't realize it at the time, this move was social suicide; both the public and her family turned against her. Her reputation as an "unfaithful wife" made people shun her without taking the time to see the beauty and intrinsic value of her art.

Just a few years prior, she had been a successful, trailblazing female artist in Korea and much admired by many forward-thinking women for her outspoken feminist writings. Now, her contemporaries turned against her; galleries would not exhibit her paintings, and she eventually died in obscurity. However, she is making a comeback in the twenty-first century. Modern art aficionados are appreciating her paintings anew and recognizing her unique talents. Her body of literature is also being read and appreciated by a new generation of feminists.

Na Hye-seok's desire to transcend the strict gender codes of her time caused her to lose everything, but without daring women like her, girls and women will never fully gain their freedom and power.

Georgette Chen—Doyenne of Paintings

Georgette Chen, born Chang Liying, was a rare and highly accomplished artist in a world dominated by Western men. What makes her accomplishments even more remarkable is that she was a Chinese woman expressing her artistry in Paris during a time when there were few Asians in Europe.

Her father was a businessman who dealt in antiques and Asian art. He moved his family to Paris in 1914 following the Chinese Revolution of 1911. Young Liying was only eight; she quickly became fluent in French and was educated in France and America. She later studied art at the Art Students' League in New York, as well as the Académie Colarossi and Académie Biloul in Paris, where she was influenced by the work of Postimpressionist artists such as Paul Cézanne.

1930 was a pivotal year for Chang Liying. First, she made her debut as a professional artist with two paintings, *Nu* and *Vue sur La Seine aux Andelys* (*View of the Seine at Les Andelys*), at the Salon d'Automne exhibition, which also showed the works of Picasso, Matisse, and Cézanne. Second, she married the love of her life, Eugene Chen, who was a diplomat and a great admirer and supporter of her art. Chang Liying changed her name to Georgette Chen after her marriage.

They were a cosmopolitan couple who traveled widely and socialized with many politically influential people of the time. Eventually, they moved to Shanghai. Due to her husband's work as a diplomat and his anti-Japanese activities, they were placed under house arrest by the Japanese when the Sino-Japanese War broke out. Eugene became ill during their confinement and died in 1944.

Georgette Chen did marry again a few years later, but the marriage didn't last. After the divorce, she settled in Singapore and devoted her life to art. Throughout her career, she exhibited widely in galleries around the world. Initially, her paintings reflected influences from many Postimpressionists and Fauvists, such as Maurice Utrillo, Paul Cézanne, and Vincent van Gogh. Later, when she settled in Singapore, she was part of the movement that established the Nanyang Style. This art movement used Western-style painting techniques to depict artistic subjects indigenous to Southeast Asia, such as tropical plants or village life. She devoted the rest of her life to painting and teaching. In Singapore, Georgette Chen is honored as a modern art pioneer who mentored and supported other artists.

Anita Magsaysay-Ho—Champion of Filipinas

As children, Anita and her two siblings spent their summers in Zambales, a coastal agricultural province in the Philippines known for mangoes, rice, and root crops. She went fishing with her mother among the mangroves, joined her brother Mike in pulling in the fishermen's nets, and tried her hand at mending them. The kids picked native fruits like mangoes and calamansi, planted flowering shrubs, gathered chicken eggs, and played with the children of local farmers.

Those happy summer days imbued young Anita Magsaysay with a deep sense of place and culture that would influence her art for the rest of her life. During her many decades as a painter, she never departed from illustrating Filipinas and their daily tasks. Although she traveled widely and led a cosmopolitan life, at heart, she strongly identified with the simplicity and strength of the women from her home country. Through her paintings, she revealed the quiet dignity and grace of these female figures, whether harvesting crops, fishing, or gathering at the market square.

In 1943, she married Robert Ho, a shipping executive. They had five children and moved constantly due to Robert's work: they lived in Brazil, Canada, Hong Kong, New York, Washington, DC, and Japan, to name a few, and lived in over thirty different houses. Despite being a busy mother and constantly relocating, she always had a studio and continued to paint.

Anita Magsaysay-Ho went on to become a member of the illustrious group of modernist artists known as the "Thirteen Moderns" of Art and the only female included. She has an unwavering love of the Philippines and a deep respect for the female form, the essence of women, and what they do every day to uphold their community and society.

Anita Magsaysay-Ho painted into her ninth decade and passed away in 2012 at ninety-seven. She is considered one of the six most outstanding painters in Filipino history.

Yayoi Kusama—Obsessed with Polka Dots, Pumpkins and Infinity

"Every time I have had a problem, I have confronted it with the ax of art."

—Yayoi Kusama

Yayoi Kusama is a wonder: she has turned her obsessions with polka dots and childhood traumas into canvases and sculptures that sell for millions of dollars at auction, not to mention becoming one of the most successful artists of the twenty-first century *after* turning sixty.

It all started when she experienced hallucinations of dots and the shapes of gourds as a child growing up on her family's seed farm in rural Japan. These unusual visions served to provide inspiration for her later creations.

She drew obsessively, and though her parents disapproved of her artistic propensities, she kept at it. Her parents had an unhappy marriage, and she was tasked by her mother to spy on her philandering husband. The young and innocent Yayoi secretly followed her father and witnessed him involved in a sex act with a strange woman. This distressing encounter led to a lifelong fear of sex. Art was her means of self-therapy and escape.

She attended the Kyoto School of Arts and Crafts and devoted all her time to art. She later sent a letter and a few watercolors to Georgia O'Keeffe. The renowned artist wrote back and encouraged her to come to America but did warn her about the difficulty of making it as an artist.

In 1958, at twenty-seven, Kusama headed for New York. Once she settled in, she received little attention for her work because she was both a woman and a Japanese person in post-World War II America. Regardless, she was very prolific, and during this period, she began painting her now iconic "Infinity Nets" series, taking inspiration from the vastness of the ocean. This image was particularly meaningful to her since she had grown up by the sea. In these works, she would obsessively paint small loops onto a monochrome white canvas, covering the entire surface from edge to edge.

In the late '60s and early '70s, Kusama began staging naked "Happenings." Instead of painting on canvases, she painted on nude volunteers. She used this sensational artistic expression to protest the Vietnam War. Some of these "Happenings" made it into the news. By this time, her pieces were being shown in European and New York galleries, but she was still barely making a living with her art.

Kusama connected with the most avant-garde personalities of the time, such as Andy Warhol, and was at the forefront of the cultural revolution of the 1970s. However, the success that she craved was blocked by sexism and subtle racial prejudice, even amongst the so-called "liberal" crowd, and white men dominated the art scene. Not only was her highly original art never fully appreciated, but several white male artists who had copied her ideas received accolades while her own creations were sidelined.

Kusama became so depressed that she attempted suicide by jumping out of her apartment window. Luckily, she landed on a bicycle and survived the fall. Wholly defeated by her experience in New York and sinking into deep depression as well as struggling with OCD, she returned to Japan in 1972. She eventually checked herself into Seiwa Hospital, a mental institution (where she still lives).

Then, in 1989, everything changed when art curator Ann Munroe found her work and asked Kusama to exhibit at the Center for International Contemporary Arts in Manhattan. Seventeen years after she had left New York in a state of emotional anguish, "Yayoi Kusama: A Retrospective" took the city and the international art scene by storm. She was rediscovered, and in 1993, the Venice Biennale (dubbed the "Olympics of the art world") invited Kusama to participate representing Japan. In 1998, "Love Forever: Yayoi Kusama, 1958–1968," which spotlighted Kusama's New York years, opened at the Museum of Modern Art in that city.

Her many canvases of polka dots, giant sculptures of pumpkins (rendered with polka dots), and infinity mirror rooms attract millions of visitors and are highly sought after by collectors. Her art pieces, which galleries could not sell in the 1970s, are now worth millions. Based on museum admissions, she is the most successful living artist and the most successful female artist of all time. Her work is held in the collections of the world's largest museums, including the Museum of Modern Art in New York and the Tate Modern in London, and her Infinity Mirrored

Rooms are extremely popular, drawing visitors in lines with often hour-long waits.

Kusama also has her own museum in Japan; tickets are sold months in advance. Located in her hometown of Matsumoto, it opened the year she turned eighty-eight. According to ARTnews, Kusama's auction sales have increased more than tenfold, from $9.3 million in 2009 to $98 million in 2019.

> *"Since my childhood, I have always made works with polka dots. Earth, moon, sun, and human beings all represent dots, a single particle among billions."*
>
> **—Yayoi Kusama**

Anida Yoeu Ali—Reimagining Possibilities Through Textile

Anida Yoeu Ali describes herself as a performance artist, poet, and global agitator. Her brilliant use of fabric in several of her most provocative art installations has a direct connection to her childhood. In 1975, when Vietnam invaded her home country of Cambodia, she and her family had to flee with literally nothing but the shirts on their backs. Eventually, they settled in Chicago, where she attended the University of Chicago and went on to earn an MFA from the Art Institute of Chicago. She considers textiles to be an extension of her skin and a way to extend her body into public space, as well as a storytelling device providing the artist the opportunity to assume different personas to interact with an audience.

Picture this: Ali pops her head through the fitted hole of a 100-meter-long tube made of saffron-colored fabric and loops, and a helper crawls into the other end of the tube to act as the tail. Now, imagine this giant caterpillar-like entity moving through a busy city street, a cafeteria, or a schoolyard. This is the *Buddhist Bug*, a phantasmagorical living art piece that has become one of Anida Yoeu Ali's most popular and iconic creations. She has displayed it around the world in the most unlikely places. It first appeared when Anida returned to Cambodia; she used it to juxtapose the changing landscapes of rural and metropolitan areas experiencing rapid development and loss of cultural identity as globalization creeps in. This recurring theme in her art is inspired by her fascination with Buddhism and the exploration of migration and impermanence.

Another of her eye-catching installations featuring colorfully opulent fabric is *The Red Chador*. For Ali, the chador is more than simply an item of clothing: it is a symbol of the struggles of Muslim women and a way to raise consciousness about the global rise of Islamophobia, misogyny, and racism. Premiering at the Palais de Tokyo museum in Paris in 2015, the series has since appeared around the world, including live performances in Hong Kong, Kuala Lumpur, Seattle, Washington, DC, and San Francisco.

Ali has won international acclaim for her work, and she has received grants from the Rockefeller Foundation, the Ford Foundation, the National Endowment of the Arts, and the Art Matters Foundation. In 2024, her solo show "Hybrid Skin, Mythical Presence" was on view at the Seattle Asian Art Museum, marking the first time a Cambodian American artist had been shown there in the museum's ninety-year history.

*"As with most of my performance personas—they are
always heroines and larger-than-life figures—women who
are bold, courageous, and unapologetic. The personas I
create transcend confinement and ideas that are rooted in
any kind of absolutism because they are hybrid forms, mixing
and matching, reinventing and reimagining possibilities."*

—Anida Yoeu Ali

Toshiko Takaezu—Poetry in Clay

In a 2009 interview, Toshiko Takaezu shared that while working on one
of her large pieces on the potter's wheel, she felt an overwhelming urge
to just dive right in. For her, the feeling of oneness with creation and
nature was key to her art. Takaezu was an incredible artist and teacher
known for helping transform the practice of ceramics from a utilitarian
craft into a true form of artistic expression. She is considered one of the
premier artists of the 1950s and '60s, one who revolutionized the use
of clay in works of abstract expressionism through which she made her
inner musings manifest.

Toshiko Takaezu was born in Hawaii to parents who immigrated from
Okinawa, Japan. She was the sixth child of eleven and grew up helping
her parents on their farm. While still in high school, she had to get a
job to help support her large family and serendipitously found one at
the Hawaiian Potter's Guild. It was a commercial place that cranked
out gaudy pieces, but it introduced her to the world of clay and glazing.
From this early encounter with how pottery is made, she rose to become
one of the most respected ceramists in the world.

After attending painting classes at the Honolulu Academy of Arts, Takaezu studied ceramics with Claude Horan at the University of Hawaii. She then moved to the mainland to attend the Cranbrook Academy of Art in Bloomfield Hills, Michigan. This academy was a hotbed of experimental art forms that fired her creative imagination; from this starting point, she combined the Western aesthetic of the arts and crafts movement with deep cultural nuances from her Japanese heritage, which included Zen Buddhism and *chanoyu* (the tea ceremony tradition).

Toshiko Takaezu ceramic works are in shapes like human hearts, torsos, mysterious cylinders, and large spheres she called "moons." Each piece is finished with her signature "closed form:" before sealing each pot, she placed a small clay bead wrapped in paper inside so the pieces would produce a rattling sound when moved. For her, the empty space within each piece holds the greatest significance, symbolizing her belief that what lies within a person is what truly matters. Friends who visited her studio would sometimes see Takaezu using her kilns to bake chicken in clay and to dry mushrooms, apples, and other harvests from her garden. In essence, there was no separation between nature, art, and the artist in her mind.

In addition to working with clay, Takaezu is also known for her paintings, weaving, and bronze sculptures. As a teacher, she has trained and inspired generations of young artists at the Cleveland Institute of Art, Princeton University, and other institutions.

In 1987, she was named a Living Treasure of Hawaii and received the National Living Treasure Award from the University of North Carolina in 1994. She also received the Konjuhosho Award in 2010, conferred by the Emperor of Japan on individuals who have made significant contributions to Japanese society. In addition, Takaezu has been awarded numerous grants, and her work has been exhibited in major museums around the world such as the Metropolitan Museum of Art, the Smithsonian American Art Museum, and the National Museum of Modern Art in Kyoto.

After many decades of living in New Jersey, Toshiko Takaezu returned to Hawaii and died there at the age of eighty-eight in 2011. She was instrumental in transforming the element of earth into modernist ceramic art that is timeless and universal.

Pacita Abad—the World Was Her Canvas

In her fifty-eight years on Earth, Pacita Abad traveled to sixty-two countries and took up residency in eleven cities, and her art has been shown in over thirty-two museums around the world. She was a creative force who was also very disciplined and prolific, leaving behind a legacy of over 5,000 pieces of colorful and provocative art pieces to inspire countless generations.

Born in 1946 in the remote town of Batanares, Philippines, she was the fifth in a family of eleven children, and both her parents were involved in education and politics. Her father and mother served in the Filipino Congress, and her brother also later became a congressman. Abad also became involved in social activism; she and her friends protested against the rigged election confirming the continued sway of dictator Ferdinand Marcos, causing her family home to be targeted by a barrage of bullets from thugs hired by Marcos to scare those opposing his autocratic rule. As a result, her parents urged her to continue her education in Spain, and in 1971, she left for Europe—but she made a stop in San Francisco which completely changed the course of her life.

The nineteen-year-old arrived the year before the Summer of Love, as psychedelic exploration and Bohemian creativity made the city a place of creative ferment, and she immediately immersed herself in the progressive culture and decided to stay. She supported herself, working as a secretary by day and a seamstress by night, while also pursuing her studies to become a lawyer. She fell in love with an artist named George Kleinman and married him; the marriage only lasted a year, but it did introduce Abad to the world of painting, which opened new possibilities for her.

In 1973, she met Jack Garrity, a development economist who was planning to travel the world before starting his professional life. She joined him, and they embarked on an extraordinary overland journey, hitchhiking their way across Asia before making a water crossing to the Philippines and onwards, a journey during which they visited Turkey, Iran, Afghanistan, Pakistan, India, Sri Lanka, Myanmar, Thailand, Laos, Taiwan, and Hong Kong. This odyssey drastically changed her life and career plans, and she decided to take up painting instead of law. She and Garrity also became husband and wife, and together, they traveled the world for his work and she created art wherever they went.

Abad once described herself as a "glutton for the visual" as she had a desire to take everything in, a trait that is strongly reflected in every piece of her art. Her pieces are bold, eclectic, multitextured, and almost impossible to put into any category, and they are always held together by her unrestrained use of color. Her themes are often infused with powerful sociopolitical nuances inspired by the struggles of the indigenous communities she encountered in her travels. She often highlighted the many horrific consequences of war and conflict, such as displacement, hunger, and oppression.

In the late 1970s and early 1980s, Abad introduced a quilting technique to her canvases, layering them with objects like stones, sequins, glass, buttons, shells, mirrors, and printed textiles. She called this "trapunto painting," and it became a defining technique for which she is famous.

Her last major work was finished while she was undergoing chemotherapy for cancer. She decided to spruce up the rather drab fifty-five-meter-long Alkaff Bridge spanning the Singapore River. Despite her illness, she managed to paint vibrant and colorful circles onto the structure, helped by volunteers. The painted bridge was formally inaugurated on January 29, 2004. Abad lived long enough to see the people of Singapore delight in the bridge makeover that transformed a utilitarian structure into a symbol of art and community. She passed away in December of that same year. Pacita Abad's work is now in public and private art collections in over seventy countries.

Tiffany Chung—Mapping a Better World

Tiffany Chung creates art installations that invite the viewer to contemplate the consequences of global conflicts, environmental crises, and the plight of refugees across different times and places.

One signature modality she has employed is the use of cartography to illustrate the reality of ever-shifting boundaries drawn by forces beyond the control of ordinary people. Her interest in war-related forced migration is rooted in her experience of fleeing Vietnam with her family after the fall of Saigon in 1975.

Tiffany Chung was born in Da Nang, Vietnam in 1969. Her father was a helicopter pilot who was shot down and imprisoned. After fourteen years, he was released, and Tiffany and her family emigrated to the US.

In college, she majored in photography and art because she strongly believed in the ability of art to influence culture and society. She was also determined to challenge the status quo of the art world, where men dominated and very few Asian women are acknowledged for their contributions.

Chung has returned to Vietnam several times to do research and document untold stories lost to the mayhem of war and the erosion of time. One memorable experience was being dropped off at a bus stop in the middle of nowhere, where she ended up waiting for ten hours! During the seemingly endless wait, she was joined by a chicken and a goat who kept her company. She based her studio in Saigon for a few years and collaborated with a group of young Vietnamese artists on a project exploring the previously officially erased Vietnam exodus history through re-rendering archival photographs into watercolor paintings.

In 2023, Chung created an outdoor exhibit at the National Mall in Washington, DC. It was a sprawling map of the world located next to the Vietnam Veterans Memorial, tracing the global routes of Southeast Asian emigrés and refugees from the Vietnam War. This provocative earthwork, entitled *For the Living*, prompted visitors to reflect on their own journeys of migration while remembering that people from Vietnam, Cambodia, and Laos, including the Hmong, suffered irretrievable losses.

Tiffany Chung has exhibited at many museums and biennials worldwide, including New York's Museum of Modern Art, the British Museum, the Louisiana MoMA in Denmark, Schirn Kunsthalle Frankfurt (Germany), and the Nobel Peace Center in Norway. Although she primarily identifies as an artist, she has extended her activism beyond the realm of museum exhibits to participate in academic and political discussions. She has led and been a part of numerous panels and symposia on topics such as asylum policies, decolonization, feminist issues, the climate crisis, and the importance of refugees having the right to claim and express their historical memories.

Dressed to Conquer

Vera Wang—Ageless Style

When a BBC interviewer asked Vera Wang how she has managed to keep her youthful looks, positive demeanor, and success after fifty years of being a top icon of couture fashion, Vera answered without hesitation, "A lot of sleep, vodka cocktails, and hard work." She also credits her phenomenal success to failure: at sixteen, after having trained for many years as a skater, she was featured in *Sports Illustrated* as a hopeful contender for gold in the 1968 Olympics. However, she failed to qualify, and this severe disappointment caused her to emotionally tumble down a bleak black hole. Then, she found fashion.

After earning an art history degree from Sarah Lawrence College and spending a year at the Sorbonne, she got a job at *Vogue* magazine as a fashion director's assistant. She rapidly became one of the youngest fashion editors ever to work there and stayed on for seventeen years, but made her exit after she was passed over to become the editor-in-chief. She then became the fashion director at Ralph Lauren for two years before striking out on her own in 1990.

During her 1989 engagement, when she wasn't able to find a simple, elegant dress that reflected her position in the world of high fashion, she designed her own gown. Then she realized there were probably scores of other women who wanted to walk down the aisle in style. This desire to rescue would-be brides from gaudy, poofy polyester frocks prompted Vera to open her first couture wedding gown boutique in New York's Carlyle Hotel. In essence, she built her fashion empire on a long white dress, and in that endeavor, she has also redefined global ideas of beauty and elegance.

She now has boutiques worldwide, including in Australia, Sydney, Tokyo, London, and New York. Celebrities like Victoria Beckham, Halle Berry, and Ariane Grande have donned Vera's wedding gowns and slinky dresses for the red carpet. Her brand also produces eyewear, jewelry, fragrances, shoes, home decorations, housewares, and even vodka. Vera Wang's design influence has become part of pop culture. She has been referenced or made cameo appearances in TV series including *Sex in the City*, *The West Wing*, *Totally Spies*, and *Ugly Betty*, and the movie *Bride Wars*.

Guo Pei—Fantasy Couture Creator

Who would imagine that a young girl who grew up wearing drab grey Mao suits in communist China would one day have a haute couture boutique on Paris's rue de Saint-Honoré? Her gowns are not just fabric stitched together to drape over female bodies, they are works of art, or as Guo Pei describes her works, fantasy couture. She intends them to last for hundreds of years and remain beautiful and appreciated, just like a painting or sculpture made by an artistic master. To describe Guo Pei's designs as fantasy is not quite adequate, however, for they bring together art, architecture, and history, all woven into works of wearable opulence.

Guo Pei's passion for sumptuous fabrics and rich, intricate embroidery was instilled by her maternal grandmother, who was from an elite family that lived through the last remaining years of the Qing Dynasty. She had beautiful jewelry and clothing tailored from fine silks and embellished with exquisite floral designs. Sadly, generations worth of treasures and finery were destroyed when Mao's Red Guards came into power, and her grandmother was considered a "class enemy." The goal was to purge China of capitalism, decadence, and extravagance. However, memories could not be purged, and Guo Pei was able to vicariously luxuriate in the clothes her grandmother had worn by listening to her reminiscences. In secret, she also taught Guo Pei to embroider in the traditional way women had done for generations before the Cultural Revolution put a damper on artistry and refinement in clothing.

Thus, she grew up with a flair for fashion even if she and other women were only allowed to wear formless grey dresses. One of her teachers accused her of being a "capitalist" when she altered a dress to improve how it fit. Fortunately, after Chairman Mao died in 1976, China became much less oppressive as the new government of Zhou En-lai allowed more cultural and artistic freedom. This offered Guo Pei the opportunity to attend the Beijing Second Light Industry School at age nineteen, and in 1986, she became one of the first fashion design students to graduate from it.

In 2015, the world learned about her designs when the music icon Rihanna wore a golden gown made from fox fur and endless spools of gold thread that weighed fifty-five pounds and took two years to make. Images of the diva walking down the red carpet at the Met Gala went viral, and Guo Pei became known around the world.

She is the first and only designer from China to have become a guest member of the Fédération de la Haute Couture et de la Mode, the official body that recognizes couturiers of the highest level. In 2019, a gold Guo Pei dress modeled after a traditional Chinese wedding gown sold at Sotheby's for £435,000 (about half a million US dollars), the highest price ever paid for a living fashion designer's work. In 2020, her solo exhibition at the San Francisco Legion of Honor was the most attended exhibit in the museum's history.

Anna Sui—Grunge Meets Baby Doll

Anna Sui is a consummate storyteller, using a harmonious cacophony of fabrics to chronicle and influence pop culture in America and beyond. She stitches the worlds of grunge girls, hippie chicks, hula girls, British mods, rock stars, Pre-Raphaelite maidens, nomads, and cowgirls into wearable stories that are also hyper-fashionable.

When Anna was four years old, she was a flower girl for her aunt's wedding in New York. As she and her parents were driving back home to Michigan, she confidently declared that she would be a fashion designer. And she did exactly that. When she was a teenager, she combed through every *Vogue* and *Seventeen* magazine she could get her hands on with her attention laser-focused on getting into Parsons School of Design. However, once she got into her dream school, she discovered that it wasn't quite what she had expected, so when she got a job with a popular designer, she left Parsons. She realized that for her, it was more important to hone her craft in the real world.

While at Parsons, she did meet Andrew Meisel, who went on to become one of the most successful fashion photographers in the industry. They became fast friends, and he was instrumental in helping Anna by introducing her to supermodels who strutted down the catwalk wearing her works, eclectic designs fusing Bohemian, grunge, and campy counterculture together.

In 1991, when Sui launched her first collection, she wanted to dress rock stars and the fans who went to their concerts. In 2024, a constellation of luminaries, including rock stars like Debbie Harry, David Johansen of the New York Dolls, and the lead singer of Phoenix, Thomas Mar, his wife Sophia Coppola, and Marc Jacobs were all seated at the front row to view her fall collection.

With over three decades as a top designer under her figurative belt, she has stayed true to her mission while building a fashion empire that stretches from Paris to Tokyo. In 2009, Sui received the Council of Fashion Designers of America Lifetime Achievement Award.

Notably, in 2017, a retrospective was held at the Fashion and Textile Museum in London entitled "The World of Anna Sui." It was the first time an American fashion designer had been featured in a retrospective exhibit in the United Kingdom.

CHAPTER SEVEN

BRIGHT STARS—
SHEROES OF THE SILVER
SCREEN AND STAGE

During the twentieth and twenty-first centuries, Hollywood and the American music industry have dominated the world of entertainment and have set standards that have excluded artists from communities outside the norm. Asian performers have been stigmatized, especially female Asian actors, who were typecast into roles that limited their abilities to play diverse and strong characters.

From the first Chinese woman who garnered a star on the Hollywood Walk of Fame to the prima ballerina who danced for three decades as the principal dancer of the San Francisco Ballet, the women in this chapter are proof that the electromagnetic force of a brilliant star cannot be extinguished.

Anna May Wong—a Star Is Born

Very few people become what they say they want to be when they are nine, let alone become successful and admired for achieving their childhood dreams and leaving a legacy that has endured the test of time. When Wong Liu Song declared as a child that she wanted to be a famous movie star, she meant it! She even came up with her stage name, Anna May Wong, at eleven years old to show she was absolutely serious. The would-be movie star often skipped school and used her lunch money to buy tickets to the cinema in the knowledge that the silver screen was her most important teacher. In 1919, when a casting call came up for *The Red Lantern*, a movie set in China, fourteen-year-old Anna secretly auditioned and got a small part as a lantern bearer. At just seventeen, she landed her first leading role in *The Toll of the Sea* (1922), the first feature-length film made in Technicolor. This silent movie was loosely based on *Madame Butterfly*, but the tragic heroine, who was named Lotus Flower, was Chinese instead of Japanese.

After her debut, Anna May Wong went on to appear in over sixty movies, but the road to stardom was anything but smooth. During the 1920s, there was still deep racial prejudice against the Chinese, and although her father had been born in the US and she herself was born and raised in California, the Chinese Exclusion Act was in full force. There were also anti-miscegenation laws, which criminalized interracial marriages and the display of any sexual reference between actors of different races. Due to these unjust societal taboos, Anna May Wong often had to compete against non-Asian women for Asian parts. Those coveted leading roles would go to Caucasian actresses made up to look Asian (i.e., in yellowface), usually with their eyes taped to a slant, which was doubly offensive.

At this point, she decided to try her luck across the ocean. She headed for Europe, mastered French and German, and starred in films, plays, and even an operetta. The Europeans were much more open to and appreciative of Anna May Wong's talents and beauty. She also made a great impression in Britain, appearing with Lawrence Oliver in the play *The Circle of Chalk* (1929). While in the UK, she starred in her last silent film, *Piccadilly* (1929). She garnered tremendous acclaim for her role, one that is often considered her best performance.

While in Germany, Anna May Wong met Marlena Dietrich and they became lifelong friends. Both were strong women with a flair for edgy fashion and exuded a dangerous sexuality that was beguiling and threatening to the status quo. They both had leading parts in the highly acclaimed *Shanghai Express* (1934), shot in Hollywood and directed by the legendary Josef von Sternberg.

By the mid-1930s, Wong had become a successful actress and fashion icon in both Europe and America. Her flamboyant yet meticulous flapper style was so popular that in 1934, the Mayfair Mannequin Society of New York voted her "The World's best-dressed woman." In today's parlance, she had become a global fashionista phenom!

During World War II, Anna May Wong spent much of her time and money supporting the Chinese against the Japanese invasion of China. She was also very outspoken about the racial inequalities that were rampant in Hollywood. After two decades in film, she began to suffer from depression and self-medicated with too many cocktails. However, she pulled herself together and made another unprecedented achievement. This time, she became the first Asian American lead in a TV show, *The Gallery of Madame Liu-Tsong*. Ten shows were produced, and Wong was featured as Madame Liu, who was an art dealer and detective. Sadly, no copies of the series have survived. Anna May Wong was awarded a star on the Hollywood Walk of Fame in 1960.

Michele Yeoh—and the Winner Is...

Anna May Wong paved the way for other Asian actresses who would shine on the silver screen. However, it would take a century after her pioneering first—a leading role in *The Toll of the Sea*—for an actress of Asian heritage to be officially celebrated as a leading thespian.

In 2023, Michele Yeoh, born in Malaysia, became the first Asian female to win the Academy Award for Best Actress for her role in *Everything Everywhere All at Once*. What's especially remarkable about Yeoh is that she was sixty when she received the golden Oscar statue.

Young Michele wanted to become a ballerina and even went to England to study at the London School of Dance when she was fifteen, but a back injury derailed her dancing career. When she returned home in 1978, her mom encouraged her to enter the Miss Malaysia contest, and Michele won. From there, she leaped into acting roles in movies that featured martial arts. She turned her naturally strong physique and the sense of discipline she'd gained from ballet into graceful fighting moves that thrilled audiences. She even did her own stunts!

Yeoh gained international fame when she became the first actress to break away from the typical Bond girl mold by playing a super-agent with brains, beauty, and kickass fighting skills opposite Pierce Brosnan's 007 in *Tomorrow Never Dies*. After the heightened celebrity status from her appearance in a Bond movie, Yeoh had many lucrative offers, but she wouldn't let herself be typecast just as an Asian femme fatale who fights and refused roles that boxed her in.

The pivotal role came in 2000 when she was cast in *Crouching Tiger, Hidden Dragon*, directed by Ang Lee. The film was a phenomenal artistic and financial success; at the 2001 Academy Awards, it swept with Oscars for Best Picture, Best Foreign Language Film, Best Art Direction, Best Original Score, and Best Cinematography. Yeoh was also nominated for a BAFTA Award for Best Leading Actress. A string of Hollywood-produced films followed, including *Memoirs of a Geisha* (2005), *Reign of Assassins* (2010), and *The Lady* (2011), in which she portrayed Burmese politician, diplomat, and activist Aung San Suu Kyi.

Then came her dazzling performance in the outrageously original science fiction/comedy multiverse of *Everything Everywhere All at Once* (2022), leading to Yeoh becoming the first Asian actress ever to win the Academy Award for Best Actress. What's truly inspiring and remarkable is that she used her heightened celebrity platform not just to promote herself but to bring attention to the plight of women and girls in areas of conflict and social disparity.

This is part of Yeoh's presentation as a Good Will Ambassador of the United Nations Development Program shortly after the 2023 Oscars:

I'm sixty years old, and I just won my first Oscar. I know something about perseverance, and I am all too aware of what society expects of women. I'm also well aware that my experience can't compare at all with that of the women heroes I've met who are on the front lines of crises. But if I can do one thing with this moment of my professional joy, it would be to point the spotlight on those who all too often go unacknowledged, the women who are rebuilding their communities, taking care of children and older people, and putting food on the table. Let's make sure they are not missing from the room when decisions are being made that affect them the most.

To top things off, in 2024, Michele Yeoh was also awarded the
Presidential Medal of Honor by President Joe Biden. The Presidential
Medal of Freedom, presented annually, is the nation's highest
civilian honor, bestowed on individuals "who have made exemplary
contributions to the prosperity, values, or security of the United States,
world peace, or other significant societal, public or private endeavors,"
per the White House.

Ali Wong—She Does It All

This groundbreaking artist has used her sharp wit and enormous
talent for satirical comedy to carve a distinctive artistic style, which
includes directing, producing, writing for numerous shows, acting,
publishing a bestseller, and motherhood. She is the very definition of a
multihyphenate: someone who works in many capacities, especially in
the field of entertainment!

Ali Wong began her career as a stand-up comedian and quickly rose to
fame with her wit and unabashed performances. She was born in San
Francisco in 1982, the youngest of four children. Her mother, a social
worker, is originally from Vietnam, and her father, an anesthesiologist,
is Chinese American. After graduating from UCLA with a degree in
Asian Studies, Wong traveled to Vietnam to learn Vietnamese and to
gain a better understanding of her Asian heritage. When she returned to
the states, she courageously jumped into stand-up comedy.

Defiantly resisting the stereotype that says all Asian women are subdued
and quiet, Ali Wong found her revelatory voice as a stand-up comedian
and worked really hard to hone her skills in New York City. She did
as many as nine gigs a night, and her reward was being voted one of
Variety's top ten comedy acts to watch in 2011.

From there, she continued to forge ahead with writing scripts and acting. In her first film role, she worked with none other than the great director Oliver Stone in *Savages* (2012). Although the movie did not do well at the box office, it gave Ali recognition and an entry into further work in films. In 2014, Wong landed a role as Dr. Lark in the ABC medical drama series *Black Box* opposite Vanessa Redgrave and Kelly Reilly.

In 2016, her provocative and brazen comedy, *Baby Cobra*, which she performed while she was six months pregnant, skyrocketed her career into hyperdrive. She wanted to highlight the fact that being pregnant is an asset and that a pregnant woman can be very powerful and creative. This breakout Netflix performance was so successful that Ali Wong became known as the "queen" of Netflix and gained millions of fans through the platform.

In addition to everything she's accomplished, she wrote the instant bestseller *Dear Girls: Intimate Tales, Untold Stories and Advice for Living Your Best Life* in 2019, while she was pregnant with her second daughter. Her inspiration in writing the book was for it to be a life guide for her daughters to read when they reach adulthood. *Dear Girls* went on to win the 2019 Goodreads Choice Award for Humor.

In *Dear Girls*, Wong says:

> My dream of having four children was replaced by utter gratitude that I was able to get pregnant three times and give birth to two beautiful girls, who exhaust me spiritually, financially, and emotionally.

In 2024, Ali Wong won the Best Actress award at the Emmys for her role in the Netflix series *Beef*, playing Amy Lau, a successful entrepreneur living the "perfect" life while inwardly finding herself spiraling out of control after a road rage incident involving a down-and-out construction worker played by acclaimed actor Steven Yuen. Ali Wong became the first Asian female to receive that honor and won a Golden Globe Award for the same role.

Awkwafina—Not Afraid to Be Awkward

Nora Lum, who performs under the name Awkwafina, is not afraid to speak her mind. In 2012, she combined her love for rap with her gift for unabashed self-expression and created the uninhibited, ribald, comedic hip-hop song "My Vag." On a whim, she posted the video on YouTube, where it went viral!

> *My vag like an operatic ballad*
> *Your vag like Grandpa's cabbage*
> *And my vag, effortless*
> *Your vag post ads on Craigslist…*

Her rhapsodic rhyme about her genitalia opened the world to her, and fame and fortune have come her way ever since. This multi-talented performer was born in Queens, New York, to parents of Chinese and Korean heritage. After her mother passed away when she was only four, her Chinese grandparents helped to raise her. Her grandma Powah's strong character and raunchy sense of humor had a lasting influence on her. After growing up in Queens, she double majored in women's studies and journalism at the University of Albany (SUNY), graduating in 2011.

Although her YouTube video of her song had gone viral, not everyone appreciated her artistic endeavor. She was fired from her publicist job when her employers realized that she was the creator and star of "The

Vag." After getting a job as a cashier in a vegan grocery store, she was invited to try doing stand-up comedy. She quickly gained popularity and released her debut album *Yellow Ranger* in 2014, before appearing on the MTV comedy series *Girl Code* (2014–2015). She then expanded into acting in films, with supporting roles in major Hollywood movies alongside cinematic superstars like Cate Blanchett and Sandra Bullock in *Ocean's Eight* (2018) and Michele Yeoh in *Crazy Rich Asians* (2018). Then, in 2019, she was cast in a leading role in *The Farewell*: "Billi," the granddaughter of a Chinese family matriarch dying of cancer. In the role, she played an American-raised granddaughter trying to negotiate the sentiments of Chinese people in China, and her portrayal of the dynamics between family members won her the Best Actress award at the Golden Globes in 2019, the first Asian actress to receive that award. She also gained a positive reception for her supporting role as a thoroughly modern BFF turned badass archer in the Marvel Cinematic Universe superhero flick *Shang-Chi and the Legend of the Ten Rings* (2021).

But what's with the "Awkwafina" moniker? It was given to her by a friend in high school, and it just stuck. Awkwafina says of her stage name, "I was looking for a pretty stupid name; I just thought it was a funny name. And it was fitting that it had 'awkward' in it because I am awkward."

As befitting an accomplished comedic actress, Awkwafina was invited to host Saturday Night Live in 2018, making her only the second Asian woman to be so honored. When she stepped onto the set, she immediately mentioned that the first Asian woman to take the stage to host SNL had done so eighteen years before. A very young Nora Lum had stood in line for hours, hoping against hope to get in and see Lucy Liu do her monologue on stage.

"My every birthday wish was, 'I want to someday be on TV.' "

—Awkwafina

Lucy Liu—Angel, Actress, Artist, and Advocate

Lucy Liu is a gifted actress known for her elegant style, beauty, and enormous artistic and creative range. Her breakout role, which made her a superstar, was as one of the "heavenly" detective trio in *Charlie's Angels* (2000) and its sequel, *Charlie's Angels: Full Throttle* (2003). Lucy's fame following her turn in the 2003 film remake of the classic '70s series landed her an appearance on Saturday Night Live, and she became the first Asian woman to host the famed late-night comedy show.

It seems clear that Liu was destined to be a star. During her senior year in college, when she auditioned for a supporting role in *Alice in Wonderland*, she unexpectedly got the lead role, traditionally played by a blond, blue-eyed female. This acting debut marked the beginning of her career as an actress who has transcended stereotypes.

In the past two decades, Liu has appeared in a remarkable array of films and TV series and has voiced roles in over twenty-five animated Disney movies. In addition, she has also expanded into directing; in the highly successful CBS series *Elementary*, which ran for seven seasons (2012–2019), she not only played the female version of Dr. Watson opposite Jonny Lee Miller's Sherlock, she also directed several episodes.

What is less known about Lucy Liu is that she is also a highly accomplished artist who works in many artistic media, including collage, paint, silkscreen, and even works made with found objects. Her artistic creations have been featured in numerous gallery exhibitions and international shows and are included in many important private collections.

Lucy Liu has also been a UNICEF Ambassador since 2004 and has traveled on missions to Lesotho, Pakistan, the Democratic Republic of Congo, Russia, Cote d'Ivoire, Egypt, Peru, and Lebanon to advocate for children's and women's issues. In 2014, she scripted and directed a short film called *Meena* to highlight three ongoing global crises: gender-based violence, maternal mortality, and sex trafficking.

> "We have the power to act—for good, for change, and most importantly, for the children of the world. The call for more action is urgent, as their rights need to be realized every day, everywhere."
>
> —Lucy Liu

Sandra Oh—It Takes a Strong Woman

A young runaway who becomes an accomplished poet and writer (*The Diary of Evelyn Lau*); a fiery and determined surgeon (*Grey's Anatomy*); an international spy hunting down a psychotic assassin (*Killing Eve*)—all of these characters have been brought to life by Sandra Oh, demonstrating to the world that she is one of the most accomplished and versatile actresses today. A thread of commonality that links all her roles is her portrayal of strong women ready to face obstacles and overcome them, reflecting her essence in real life.

Sandra Mijiu Oh's parents immigrated to Canada from South Korea
and had three children, two girls and one boy. Sandra was born in
1971; her middle name, Mijiu, means "beautiful pearl." When she was
around four, her parents sent her to ballet school to correct her pigeon
toes. Those dancing lessons not only cured her gait, they unleashed her
passion for performing. She got her first acting role in *The Canadian
Geese* at age ten. A few years later, instead of accepting a scholarship
to study journalism, Sandra Oh enrolled in the prestigious National
Theatre School of Canada, a move she made much to her parents'
dismay since they did not consider acting a bona fide career. But
Sandra knew what she wanted and paid her own way to study to pursue
her passion.

At nineteen, right out of theater school, she was chosen from over
a thousand other actresses auditioning to play the leading role of a
struggling Chinese poet in *The Diary of Evelyn Lau.* Shortly after, she
also snagged the leading role in *Double Happiness*, a film about a young
aspiring actress defying the strict control of her Chinese immigrant
parents. Oh received critical acclaim for both these roles, and her
portrayal of Evelyn Lau brought her a Gemini Awards nomination
(formerly Canada's equivalent of the Academy Awards) as well as the
1994 Cannes FIPA d'Or award in the Best Actress category.

In 1996, Oh decided to give Hollywood a try and crossed the border
from Canada to the states, but her first seasons in Tinseltown weren't
easy. She was so broke that she couldn't pay rent and survived on sweet
potatoes and pizza. Then she won the lottery! Yes, really. It was a modest
win of $5,000, but that paid the rent and allowed her to stay long enough
to land two roles that year. She had a small part in Rowan Atkinson's
comedy movie *Bean* and played an ongoing role in the darkly comedic
sitcom *Arliss*, that of Rita Wu, the smart and sassy personal assistant

to a scheming sports agent. The show ended up running for six years, 1996 to 2002.

Sandra Oh also starred in the road comedy *Sideways* (2004) and the long-running TV drama *Grey's Anatomy*. In 2018, her portrayal of Eve Polastri, a British intelligence officer chasing after an elusive international female assassin, received wide acclaim, and she won both a Golden Globe and an Emmy for Best Leading Actress. She is the first actress of Asian heritage to win those coveted awards and to host the Golden Globe Awards.

Her many outstanding performances have garnered her so many awards that it's hard to keep track. In addition to her Emmy and two Golden Globe Awards, Sandra Oh has also won four Screen Actors Guild Awards, and in 2019, she made *Time* magazine's list of the 100 most influential people in the world. She has become a role model for other Asian actresses as she has continued to receive accolades for her charismatic performances and has branched out into producing. In 2023, Oh partnered with Awkwafina in a provocative performance in the comedy *Quiz Lady*, a story of two sisters on their way to a game show.

Oh is also an outspoken activist against Asian hate. In 2021, she spoke at an anti-hate rally in Pittsburgh right after eight Asian women were shot and killed by a white male mass shooter in Atlanta, Georgia, delivering a passionate, powerful speech ending with, "I am proud to be Asian! I belong here!"

Besides being the first Asian woman to accomplish so many firsts in an industry still dominated by residual sexism and racial bias, Sandra Oh is a first-class thespian. She captivates audiences with her magnificent performances, which can make people laugh and cry within the delivery of a single line.

Joan Chen—from Shanghai to International Stardom

The first few years of Joan Chen's childhood in Shanghai were very happy and privileged as her grandparents and parents were scholars and doctors educated in England and America. But with Chairman Mao's imposition of new restrictions aimed at purging "bourgeois elements" from communist China in 1966, her life—and that of millions of others across China—was changed forever. Anyone who was Western-educated was suspected of being a spy and a counterrevolutionary. When accused, Joan's beloved maternal grandfather, who was a renowned neuropharmacologist, refused to confess to crimes he did not commit and killed himself under the pressure. Five-year-old Joan was suddenly surrounded by grief amid the descending darkness of the Cultural Revolution.

Practically overnight, five other families moved into the Chen family's ancestral home, and young Joan and her family were crowded into two small bedrooms that also doubled as daytime living areas and a makeshift kitchen. Joan shared one bedroom with her grandmother, while her brother and her parents squeezed into another bedroom. Her grandmother, who was naturally audacious and brilliant, hid "counterrevolutionary" contraband in a suitcase and brought it out to entertain and educate Joan in secret. Their one-room abode became a sanctuary: Joan learned English from her grandmother's Linguaphone records and was enchanted by her colorful recounting of plays she had seen in the West End or on Broadway as they flipped through treasured playbills together.

When Joan Chen reached her late teens, her brilliant good looks were noticed, and the communist propaganda machine turned her into a teen star in films that glorified communism to promote the agenda of the Cultural Revolution. She became the "national darling" and communist poster girl for Mao's government. Because of her star status and usefulness to the cause, she was never sent to do hard labor in the countryside at a time when most of her peers were. Eventually, her parents managed to get government-sanctioned grants to study in America, and after much finagling, she was able to join them in 1981.

In America, Chen was a nobody—just another immigrant—since no one knew she was a star in China. She started college and was working in a restaurant one day when someone suggested that she should get an agent to represent her in the US. As soon as she did, calls for auditions began coming in.

She auditioned for a particular role in 1986 but was turned down because as it turned out, they were looking for someone Hawaiian. However, Chen's natural beauty and talent could not be suppressed. As she was leaving that audition and walking through the parking lot feeling dejected, a car pulled up beside her and a mysterious old man rolled down his tinted window and approached her, managing to hand her his business card despite her initial suspicion.

The old dude was in fact Dino de Laurentis, the well-known Italian American producer of many box office hits, and he cast her in the leading female role in his movie *Tai Pan* (1986). From there, her next big break was in *The Last Emperor*, directed by legendary Italian director Bernardo Bertolucci. The film won nine Academy Awards and catapulted Joan Chen into international star status. Even so, she was still being offered stereotyped roles, and although a steady stream of on-screen work came her way, she decided to pivot to directing. Chen's first film as a director was *Xiu Xiu: The Sent Down Girl* (1998). This movie revealed the awful humanitarian disaster brought on by Mao's Cultural

Revolution. Due to the subject matter of her film, Joan was banned from China for several years after its release.

Joan Chen continues to display her magnetic screen presence in many films. Because of her experience of the Cultural Revolution and of having been banned from China due to her art and desire for freedom of expression, she is a passionate advocate for artists and the freedom to express their creativity.

After a long hiatus, Chen is riding a career renaissance. In 2024, her understated but dynamic portrayal of a mother to a teenage boy in the indie film *Didi* (directed by Sean Wang) won Chen much praise.

She is married to a cardiologist and lives in San Francisco. They have two grown daughters.

Singers

Ros Serey Sothea—the Golden Voice of Cambodia

After ninety years of colonial occupation, the French exited Cambodia in 1959, after which the young Cambodian Prince Norodam Sinhanok, himself an avid musician and songwriter, enthusiastically cultivated the development of the music and film industry in his country. In the 1960s to early '70s, the Phnom Penh music scene was the genesis of a distinctive sound that combined traditional Cambodian ballads, rock and roll, and psychedelic rock accented with French and Latin rhythms. It was in this highly creative milieu that Ros Serey Sothea found her voice, enchanting listeners across her country.

Ros was born into a family of rice farmers in 1948, and from an early age, it was clear that she had a unique vocal gift. When she was fifteen, her friends persuaded her to enter a local singing contest, and she won. Soon after, a well-known singer from the National Radio heard her voice and invited her to the capital city of Phnom Penh.

This massive National Radio exposure jumpstarted her performing career, and she collaborated with several famous male crooners of the day. At nineteen, Ros Serey Sothea married the famous Sos Mat, one of the most popular singers in Phnom Penh. But not only did he turn out to be extremely jealous and physically abusive, he also had two other wives! Fed up with her husband's misogyny, she took the courageous step of divorcing him. During the era in question, that was a bold move for a woman. It did damage her reputation, which hurt her career for a time, but her great talent could not be eclipsed. With the help of other well-known musicians, she regained her popularity despite the taboo against divorce in those days. She also started singing for the soundtracks of many movies and even starred in a few.

Tragically for her and for Cambodia, the brief decade of freedom for artists came to a crashing end when the dictator Pol Pot and the Khmer Rouge took over the country. Pol Pot's regime initiated extreme reforms, and many artists, academics, and intellectuals were executed or sent to do hard labor in the countryside to force them into following communist doctrines. Ros Serey Sothea was arrested and most likely sent to a labor camp where she eventually perished.

Most of her recordings were destroyed by the Khmer Rouge, but decades later, her hauntingly clear and beautiful voice was heard again by people around the world in the movie *City of Ghosts* (2002), directed by Matt Dillon. Thanks to this film and Cambodian rock music aficionados, Ros Serey Sothea's music has been revived and enjoyed by a new generation.

She was part of the creative force that blossomed during a unique time in Cambodia's history, and the rediscovery of her music enriches the cultural and social fabric of her country and the world.

Chhom Nimol—a Twenty-First Century "Celestial Nymph"

The lead singer for Dengue Fever is another Cambodian diva named Chhom Nimol, who covered many of Ros Serey Sothea's songs decades later. Unlike Ros, Chhom Nimol did not sing as a child in the rice fields, but she and her family were also victims of the Khmer Rouge and the brutal civil war that erupted in the 1970s. They had to flee Cambodia; for a time, they lived in refugee camps in Thailand until things improved to the point that they could return to their home country. Like Ros, in youth, Chhom showed that she already had a beautiful and clear singing voice. Her parents were also renowned folk musicians, and her older sister was already a famous singer in their country. So, at sixteen, she was encouraged to enter the Apsara Awards, a contest similar to American Idol. Although she was totally scared and nervous, she won! ("Apsara" means "celestial nymph" in Cambodian.) From there, Chhom's rise as a modern diva enchanting a brand new audience with Cambodian rock and other genres of music has been going strong since 2001.

Chhom Nimol and her band Dengue Fever are reconnecting with and honoring a bygone era in Cambodian history, something that is especially important since so many of the stars of Cambodian popular music were killed or disappeared during the rule of the Khmer Rouge, including Ros Serey Sothea.

After winning the song contest, Chhom Nimol was invited to the US by the Cambodian community in exile. She started to sing at gigs in

California, and then during a performance in 2000, she was approached by two dodgy-looking bearded white men asking her to be the lead singer of their band. At first, she was very cautious and skeptical about these two brothers, Ethan and Zac Holtzman, wanting to perform Cambodian rock. But she came to realize that these guys genuinely wanted to play this music and that she would be the perfect front woman for the band.

Since the band's inception, they have gained many fans around the world. In 2005, the band toured Cambodia and was a sensational hit. It was the first time any band, much less an American one, had performed Khmer rock in Cambodia since Pol Pot and the Khmer Rouge devastated the country in 1975. A couple years later, while touring again in Cambodia, they partnered with producer John Pirozzi to make the documentary *Dengue Fever: Sleepwalking Through the Mekong* (2007).

Chhom Nimol, who has performed regularly for the king and queen of Cambodia, is the band's center of gravity and modern-day "apsara." Her powerful singing, ornamented with masterful use of vibrato and coupled with mesmerizing moves based on traditional Cambodian dance gestures, has delighted audiences of all ages and backgrounds. In 2023, after an eight-year hiatus, Dengue Fever released a new album, *Ting Ming*.

Notably, Dengue Fever has contributed to philanthropic initiatives that benefit Cambodia, such as wildlife and forest restoration, and to Cambodian Living Arts, an organization dedicated to preserving Cambodian music that was nearly lost during the turbulent years of the country's history.

Teresa Teng—the Eternal Queen of Asian Pop

This legendary chanteuse from Taiwan has so many devoted fans around the world that stamps have been issued in her honor, including in Argentina, Liberia, Grenada, Sierra Leone, the Tuva and Sakha Republics of Russia, Papua New Guinea, Timor, Mali, North Korea, and Abkhazia, as well as Taiwan, Hong Kong, China, and Japan. Her mellifluous voice, along with her graceful persona, has touched millions of hearts.

If you look at a picture of Teresa Teng, you will see a beautiful and charming Asian woman with a sweet demeanor. However, her achievements during her life—as well as her legacy even decades after her death—are so astounding that they stand as a testament to the power of feminine beauty and artistry that can soothe and heal the soul. She was named one of the world's seven greatest female singers by *Time* magazine in 1986. Well before the days of the internet and social media, she sold over forty-eight million records during her life. She is best known as the creator of Mandopop (Mandarin pop).

Teresa Teng was born in Taiwan on January 29, 1953, to an army officer father; her mother exposed her daughter to movies and Chinese opera from a young age. When she was eleven, her mother entered her into a singing contest sponsored by a broadcasting corporation, and she won. From there, Teresa went on to become one of the most popular singers in Asia for two decades. Her live performances filled stadiums, often drawing over 100,000 fans.

Teresa Teng is celebrated as the "Queen of Asian Singing" and has captivated audiences across Asia and beyond. She sang in a diversity of languages, including Mandarin, Cantonese, Minnan dialect, Japanese, Malay, English, and Indonesian, and she played a crucial role in shaping and popularizing Chinese pop music. There's a saying that goes, "Wherever there are Chinese, there is the voice of Teresa Teng." Her voice not only defined a generation but continues to resonate with and inspire many young artists who pay tribute by covering her classic songs.

Despite her immense popularity in China, she did not hesitate to express her support for the Tiananmen rebellion. On May 27, 1989, over 300,000 people attended the concert called "Democratic Songs Dedicated to China" at the Happy Valley Racecourse in Hong Kong. One of the highlights was Teng singing "My Home Is on the Other Side of the Mountain." After her defiant performance, fearing retribution from the government of Deng Xiao Ping, she moved to France.

In 1995, while on vacation in Thailand with her French fiancé, Teresa Teng suffered a serious asthma attack and died on the way to the hospital. She was only forty-two, and her untimely death deeply shocked her legions of fans around the world. Taiwan honored her with a state funeral that drew over 200,000 mourners who lined the streets of Taipei as her coffin traveled across the city.

Decades after her death, her recordings are still hot sellers across Asia and beyond. Now, with the advancement of technology, there are even Teresa Teng hologram concerts replete with stunning stage lighting, projections, LED videos, and various dance performances and special effects.

Millions of fans from across Asia still commemorate Teresa Teng. The hotel suite at the InterContinental in Chiang Mai, the place where she passed, has been turned into a museum, and thousands of visitors visit every year. In Taiwan, her final resting place has become the Teresa Teng Memorial Park, a popular tourist destination for her fans from around the world.

Teng is also remembered for her expansively generous heart. She frequently held concerts in Singapore, Taiwan, and Hong Kong to raise funds for philanthropic causes, donating the proceeds to hospitals and charities in those places. She has even had a street named after her in Ivry-sur-Seine, in the southeastern part of Paris. The name was adopted by the vote of the Municipal Council of France in 2022.

Theresa Teng's most famous and iconic song is "The Moon Represents My Heart":

> *You ask how deeply I love you and just how great my love is;*
> *Consider this and look above: the moon represents my heart.*

Rina Sawayama—Decoding Identity Through Music

Not many musicians get to perform a duet with Sir Elton John; yet that's exactly what Rina Sawayama has accomplished! Sir Elton sat at the piano and accompanied her in singing a song she wrote, "Chosen Family." What's more, Elton John declared her album *Sawayama* his favorite for 2020.

With no formal training in music, Rina Sawayama is truly a naturally gifted musician, songwriter, and performer. Her childhood introduction to music happened during the family's many hours spent in karaoke singing. Later, at the age of twelve, young Rina convinced her father to give her a guitar after she began listening to pop punk artist Avril Lavigne. The young teen taught herself chords on it, and before long, she was writing her own songs.

Sawayama spent a few years indulging her wanderlust, but eventually enrolled at Cambridge, where she studied psychology, sociology, and politics. She used what she learned to write lyrics that explore racism, sexism, intergenerational pain, and cultural identity. After graduation, she boldly decided that she was going to be a professional musician and performer, even working three jobs in order to finance her goal. In 2013, she released her debut single, "Sleeping in Waking."

Then Sawayama went into a psychological tailspin in which she doubted everything in her life, including her identity. To reclaim her sense of self, she embarked on a journey of exploring her family history while embracing her identity as a Japanese-British pansexual woman. The introspective odyssey led to the creation of her 2020 debut album, *Sawayama*, a standout album embracing a bold fusion of pop, opera, house music, and hair metal that transforms her inner struggles into a captivating musical self-portrait. It peaked at number eighty on the UK Albums Chart, and included "Chosen Family," the song later to be performed as a duet with Elton John. It also features a track entitled "STFU!," a bold, unfiltered, explicit response to the racist and fetishizing comments she faces as a Japanese woman living in the West.

Sawayama was unable to compete for the Mercury Prize (an annual music prize awarded for the best album released by a musical act from the United Kingdom or Ireland) because she was told by the management that she wasn't "English" enough because she wasn't born in the UK. In response, she started a campaign to change the industry's outdated standards. Her unapologetic complaint about their antiquated rules helped to spark a firestorm through the UK's music and entertainment world, which brought widespread criticism that the rules were exclusionary and othering. The Mercury Prize and BRIT Awards revised their eligibility criteria to allow all UK residents to enter the prestigious music competitions.

In 2023, she landed a prize role in *John Wick: Chapter 4*. Keanu Reeves had seen her videos, and on his recommendation, she got a call from famed director Chad Stahelski. When they met, she was cast on the spot. Sawayama did her own stunts, which involved swords, knives, guns, and some serious martial art moves. Her acting in the action film was also stellar.

Rina Sawayama continues to fearlessly use her voice in her activism against misogyny, gender bias, and racial bias, especially within the music industry, all while she hones her creativity and dazzles the world with her cutting-edge music and acting. In 2024, she was honored with the Asia Entertainment Game Changer Award by the Asia Society.

Jennifer Lee (a.k.a. TokiMonsta)— Unstoppable Electronica

It's pretty scary when a professional musician loses her ability to speak and recognize music! Imagine that all sounds have become indiscernible mush, and your speech slurs out as gibberish.

That's exactly what happened to Jennifer Lee, a.k.a. TokiMonsta. This terrifying onset of acute aphasia (the inability to communicate) happened after she had to undergo two brain surgeries in 2015, when she was twenty-eight years old.

She had developed a rare disease known as Moyamoya, and the only way to manage its progression was to have the two brain operations. Fortunately for her, her resilient and courageous attitude helped her to recover within a few months, and she went back to making music. In 2019, she was nominated for a Grammy in the Electronica category for her album, *Luna Rouge*.

TokiMonsta is definitely a force to admire. The determination she brought to overcoming her life-threatening illness reflects the distinctive path that she has carved out in the world of electronic music, which is still very much dominated by men. The genre's techno-centric orientation has made it a guys-only type of thing. When TokiMonsta got started in the field, many listeners and critics assumed that she had a male collaborator helping her with all the technical and computer stuff, because how could any girl master it, right? Well, Jennifer Lee learned it all herself!

She and her younger sister were raised by their single mom, and young Jennifer became the techie in their household from an early age. She figured out how to set up the remote, set up their cable TV, and taught her mom how to use her new smartphone.

On top of stepping into the role of the family computer guru, Jennifer also trained in classical music, but when she heard hip-hop artists TLC in high school, she was hooked. Finally, in college, she set up her computer with Digital Audio Workstation (DAW) apps and all the dizzying electronic peripherals that go with them. She mastered them with obsessive determination and without any male assistance!

TokiMonsta creates music that blends her Korean heritage and Western upbringing. She also incorporates field recordings of everyday sounds such as car doors slamming, birds chirping, or waves crashing into her music, resulting in transitory soundscapes that can never be replicated. Since her recovery, she has played to rave reviews at South By Southwest (SXSW) and Coachella, gaining ever more fans and continuing to develop her bold and original style.

Yuriko Kikuchi—a Born Dancer

In 1923, the "great influenza" pandemic which had peaked a few years prior came roaring back across the western states of the US, and Yuriko Amemiya's mother sent her daughter to Japan to keep her safe from this deadly virus which had taken millions of lives, including that of Yuriko's father and two siblings. While in Japan, she started to take dance lessons, and from her first arabesque, she knew that she wanted to dance for the rest of her life.

When Yuriko returned to the US at seventeen, she furthered her dance studies with the Dorothy Lyndall Dance Company while also working as a florist. Her talents were soon noticed, and she was invited to perform with the UCLA Dance Club. This exposure led to her being selected for the lead dance role of Rima, a character from Henry Hudson's play, *The Green Mansion*, who was half bird and half human. Yuriko's performance matched Rima's haunting and beguiling nature and would have brought her many more leading roles, but on December 7, 1941, Japan's bombs dropped on Pearl Harbor and everything changed.

Yuriko, along with her mother and stepfather and over 120,000 other Americans of Japanese ancestry, was forced into internment camps. First, they were herded to a detention center near Tulare, California. She recalled the living conditions, describing it as like living in "horse stalls." Later, they were moved to the Gila River Relocation Center in Arizona. In both camps, Yuriko took the initiative to give dance lessons to the children. Even though resources were very limited, they managed to cobble together a stage and found a piano so Yuriko and her young students could perform *The Nutcracker*. It was an uplifting and healing endeavor for all the detainees.

In 1943, Yuriko was able to leave the internment camp by signing a loyalty oath to the US. She was given $25, a ticket, and a suit and headed straight for New York City. The internment camp supervisor arranged an interview for her for a job as a seamstress. However, due to laws against hiring people of Japanese descent at that time, she was initially turned away. Nevertheless, her skills as a seamstress were so strong that she was eventually hired and then quickly promoted to be the floor manager in charge of a team of workers. Yuriko became the first Japanese worker to be admitted into the International Ladies Garment Workers' Union. Years later, Yuriko would say that she "cracked the union."

Soon after settling in the Big Apple, Yuriko went to renowned choreographer Martha Graham's studio and knocked on the door. Martha Graham herself opened the door, and the meeting of these two women launched a collaboration that eventually produced some of the most dynamic and memorable performances in the world of modern dance. Yuriko became the lead dancer for Martha Graham's Dance Company in 1944 and stayed with the performing ensemble for the next fifty years.

Beyond dancing for Graham, Yuriko also performed in the original Broadway productions of The King and I and Flower Drum Song, appeared on television and in motion pictures, and taught other famous dancers such as Mikhail Baryshnikov and Reiko Sato. Yuriko also enjoyed a fulfilling marriage to George Kikuchi, and they had two children, Lawrence and Susan. Her daughter followed in her mother's footsteps and became a well-known dancer in her own right.

The Martha Hill Dance Fund honored Yuriko with a Lifetime Achievement Award in 2012, and the following year, the Japanese government awarded her the Foreign Minister's Commendation.

Yuriko was active well into her nineties and continued to teach and mentor young dancers. She passed away in 2022 at the age of 102. Her luminous and mystical stage presence will inspire generations of dancers well into the future.

Yuanyuan Tan—Always En Pointe and Elegant

One hot summer night in Shanghai, while everyone was eating salted soybeans and watermelon to stay cool, Yuanyuan Tan, watching a tiny black-and-white TV, was transfixed by the sight of Galina Ulanova dancing Swan Lake. It was her first taste of ballet.

As fate would have it, years later, the legendary Russian prima ballerina was a judge at the 1992 International Ballet Competition in Paris. Galina gave Yuanyuan Tan a perfect score for her performance, and with that high score, Tan won the competition's gold medal. Looking at Yuanyuan Tan's remarkable career as one of the most renowned ballerinas of the twenty-first century, it is apparent that she was fated to dazzle the world with her arabesques, grand jetés, and pirouettes.

When Yuanyuan was around nine, scouts from the Shanghai Dance School visited her class looking for young talents for their ballet program. They were impressed by Tan's natural physique and flexibility, and she was immediately offered a scholarship and invited to study at the school. However, her father, who wanted his daughter to become a doctor or engineer, was completely against it. Yuanyuan's mother, however, who had harbored desires of her own to become a ballerina, was overjoyed to hear of this opportunity. Her parents argued the point for months until the Shanghai Dance School officials told them that they had to make a decision "now or never" because Yuanyuan was turning eleven and further delay would make it too late. Given the ultimatum, Mr. and Mrs. Tan tossed a coin…and the unknowable mysteries of chance determined the course of Yuanyuan's life.

After completing her training in China, she received a scholarship to train at the John Cranko Schule in Stuttgart, Germany. In 1995, the director of the San Francisco Ballet, Helgi Tomasson, saw then-nineteen-year-old Tan in a ballet competition and invited her to perform as a guest artist at the ballet's Opening Night Gala. She accepted and flew to San Francisco with the intention to return to Germany after the gala to finish her training; instead, she never left. The following year, she was promoted to the rank of principal dancer, making her the youngest principal in the SF Ballet's history and the first Chinese dancer to reach this prestigious rank. She mesmerized audiences with flawless performances of classics such as *Giselle, Swan Lake*, and *The Nutcracker*, as well as dance pieces that were specially choreographed for her.

During the middle of her career, Tan suffered a serious hip injury and the doctors told her that she needed surgery, but that there was a 65 percent chance that she would not be able to dance again. Not dancing was not an option, so she took a few weeks off and sought the help of traditional Chinese medicine treatments of acupuncture and Chinese herbs along with meditation. She was back on stage after a month; she was still in pain, but her will was stronger. It took almost seven years to heal completely, but Tan never gave up on her love of dance.

Tan continued as a principal dancer until her retirement in 2024. A career spanning nearly thirty years is extremely rare in ballet as it is such a physically demanding art form. Her longevity and influence can be credited to her deep passion for ballet and her complete dedication to perfecting the steps, turns, lifts, and leaps that have made her such a *tour de force* on stage.

On Valentine's Day, February 14, 2024, she danced her last performance with the SF Ballet, performing Ashton's *Marguerite and Armand*. It was also her forty-eighth birthday.

Throughout Yuanyuan Tan's career, she has advocated for Chinese American artists in the San Francisco Bay Area, and she has received many honors and awards from cultural institutions in China and America. Her legacy—one of building bridges between the East and West—stands as a beautiful reminder that the transformative power of art is a catalyst for connection and the exchange of culture, deepening our appreciation of what it expresses.

Devi Dja—the Eternal Sunshine from Java

Devi Dja (born Misria Dja) has the distinction of being the first Indonesian woman to become a naturalized citizen of the US in 1954. Her life before settling in America is a wondrous tale of an itinerant performer who mesmerized audiences from Jakarta to London to New York and beyond.

Misria Dja was born in East Java in 1914 and raised by her grandparents, who were street musicians and managed a troupe of performers. She grew up surrounded by the sounds of the *hendang* (a two-headed drum) and the sitar and learned to sing and dance to traditional Javanese songs.

When Misria was around nine, she became seriously ill, and her name was then changed to Soetidjah (shortened to Dja). A native healer recommended the name change to protect the child from malevolent spirits. Her new name means "sun eternal;" she did recover from her illness.

Dja became a very talented singer and dancer and charmed audiences while traveling with her grandparents' troupe. At age thirteen, she attracted the attention of Willy Piedro, who managed a touring theater company called Dardanella, and he asked her to join. Eventually he also asked for her hand in marriage, and her grandparents did not stand in their way.

In the late 1920s and early 1930s, Dardanella was a hit in Southeast Asia and India. The troupe numbered nearly 150 people, including stage hands, costume makers, and performers. They performed around Southeast Asia, then India, and even journeyed to Turkey, Morocco, France, and Germany. Dja became known as "the Pavlova of the Orient" after the famous Russian ballerina Anna Pavlova. While Dardanella was touring in Europe, everything changed overnight when Hitler invaded Poland in 1939. The band of performers was stranded: they could not return to Indonesia, and they did not want to be trapped in Europe with the war approaching, so they headed west to America.

Devi Dja and her husband soon found appreciative audiences from New York to California, so they stayed on. Eventually, Dja established a dance school in Los Angeles and shared her expertise as a consultant for a few Hollywood films. Notably, she was cast as a Balinese dancer and delivered a hypnotic performance in MGM's *The Picture of Dorian Grey* (1945).

Devi Dja became the unofficial ambassador for Indonesia and was instrumental in introducing the rich aesthetic of Javanese and Balinese dance to the West. In the 1950s, Dja's studio in the Vermont area of Los Angeles became a gathering place for Indonesian artists, writers, and students. She regularly hosted soirées and social events and gained a reputation as a "godmother" to Indonesian visitors. Indonesian air force officers training in California would come visit to enjoy her *sayur lodeh* (a delicious Indonesian stew made with coconut and spices).

Devi Dja died in 1989 from cancer; her epitaph reads: "May You Dance in God's Light Forever."

CHAPTER EIGHT

ECOWARRIORS—
WOMEN PROTECTING
MOTHER EARTH

Since the publication of Rachel Carson's *Silent Spring* in 1962, environmental activists have sounded the alarm about the dangers of unchecked burning of fossil fuels, plastic production, spraying of pesticides, and the widespread use of genetically modified organism technology creating a toxic maelstrom that endangers life on Earth for all living beings. Many scientists agree that the epoch in which we live can be called the Anthropocene, an unofficial unit of geologic time used to describe negative impacts on the environment solely due to human activities.

Another term for our current state of decline is the "sixth mass extinction," in which a high percentage of existing species—bacteria, fungi, plants, mammals, birds, reptiles, amphibians, fish, and invertebrates—are dying out. If this sounds dire, it is! Is there hope for the biodiversity of planet Earth?

We need to realize that manmade destructive practices can only be undone by mankind.

Or else perhaps it is now up to womankind and the emerging power of ecofeminism to lead us out of the mire and into a new paradigm based on deep respect and care for Mother Earth.

Vandana Shiva—Defender of Seeds, Soil, and Ecofeminism

Vandana Shiva's PhD thesis when she studied at the University of Western Ontario was entitled "Hidden Variables and Non-locality in Quantum Theory," which gives you an idea of how smart she is! She holds degrees in physics and philosophy, and with her armful of academic accomplishments, she could easily have enjoyed a cushy, high-paying job anywhere in the world. Instead, she decided to focus her attention and energy on protecting the environment and has become a powerful force defending Mother Nature, protecting seeds, and introducing ecofeminism into our social consciousness.

Vandana Shiva's mother was a farmer, and her father was a forest conservationist. Her parents brought her up with a love and respect for the land and the ecosystems that support all life. Her father often brought his three children with him into the forest, where he taught them about flora and fauna and they worked together to collect cinnamon and other herbs.

As an adult, while on a visit back to her home village of Dehradun, near the foothills of the Himalayas, she was shocked to discover that a favorite forest grove by a stream had been clear-cut to make room for industrialized farming. This had a searing effect on her and was the catalyst for her to start the Research Foundation for Science, Technology, and Ecology in 1982. Despite its grand name, the foundation had a humble start: its first office was set up in her mother's cow shed. It aimed to develop sustainable methods of agriculture.

In 1991, Vandana Shiva founded Navdanya (which means nine seeds in Hindi). Its mission is to promote peace and sustainability:

> Navdanya's mission is to empower the communities belonging to any religion, caste, sex, groups, landless people, small and marginal farmers, deprived women and children, or any other needy person to ensure that they have enough to eat, they live in a healthy environment, and they are able to take action independently and effectively to become self-reliant through sustainable use of natural resources and fairness and justice in all relationships.

Navdanya is instrumental in helping farmers save heirloom indigenous seeds and has established over one hundred local seed banks around India.

In 1993, Shiva received the Right Livelihood Award, commonly known as the "Alternative Nobel Prize." Other awards she has received include the Order of the Golden Ark, the United Nations's Global 500 Award, the Earth Day International Award, the Lennon Ono Grant for Peace, and the Sydney Peace Prize in 2010. In 2003, *Time* magazine identified Shiva as an "environmental hero," and *Asia Week* has called her one of Asia's five most powerful communicators. She has also written over twenty books.

In 2022, a documentary called *The Seeds of Vandana Shiva* was released to huge acclaim. It encapsulated Shiva's decades of selfless and courageous actions for humanity and our planet.

Nadine Chandrawinata—from Beauty Queen to Ocean Defender

Nadine Chandrawinata is a well-known actress and filmmaker who won the Miss Indonesia beauty pageant in 2005. She has used her celebrity status in a poignant and powerful way to defend the ocean and all the creatures that live there. She is also a champion of gender equality.

Chandrawinata is a passionate diver. She spent so much time in the beautiful oceans surrounding Indonesia that she became acutely and unavoidably aware that plastics and other industrialized pollutants are devastating the ocean's ecology. So, in 2015, she founded the nonprofit SeaSoldier to bring attention to the dire situation. The nonprofit's four main purposes are to educate small businesses about plastic pollution, protect dolphins and their habitats, protect trees and forests, and protect mangrove ecosystems. She believes that when we protect the environment, it will protect us.

It wasn't easy for her and the organization she founded to get to where they are today. During SeaSoldier's early years, it was hard to get people to join in. "But I just went with it and never gave up," Nadine Chandrawinata recalls. "Then I decided to speak through action. I called on everyone who shares the same vision as me and who wants to make a change. Through [everything from] beach cleanings to workshops and parades, people started to notice our presence and gradually started taking part in the movement."

As a filmmaker, Nadine Chandrawinata has also used her talent to focus on the intersectionality of environmentalism and feminism. She is also the coral reef ambassador for Indonesia's Ministry of Marine Affairs and Fisheries. With over two million followers on Instagram and 30,000 followers of the #seasoldier hashtag, she is making a positive impact on future generations.

> "To me, protecting the environment is an obligation, not an option."
>
> —Nadine Chandrawinata

Oyun Sanjaasuren—an Unintentional Shero for Democracy, Women, and the Environment

There are those who succumb to a personal tragedy and suffer for years walled inside their own grief, and then there are those who transcend suffering and refocus their pain into actions that serve humanity. Oyun Sanjaasuren is a woman who has transcended.

In 1998, her beloved brother, Zorig Sanjaasuren, was killed while running a campaign to bring democratic reform to Mongolia. Only in his early twenties, he had been instrumental in ending one-party rule in Mongolia and bringing a semblance of free election to the country. He became Minister of Infrastructure and was slated to become the next prime minister but was brutally slain in his apartment by two assassins. Oyun Sanjaasuren was working overseas when she learned of her brother's death. She immediately left her well-paid job and her comfortable life in London, returned to Ulaanbaatar (previously Ulan Bator), and made the momentous decision to carry on her brother Zorig's legacy.

She earned a master's in geochemistry from Charles University in Prague and a doctorate in geology from Cambridge University. In addition to Mongolian, she is fluent in Russian, English, and Czech. Although she was not a politician, she fearlessly stepped into her brother's position. She won his parliamentary seat and later became Minister of Foreign Affairs and Minister of Environment and Green Development. When Oyun Sanjaasuren entered the Mongolian parliament, there were only three women among more than seventy-five men. Since her election, the number of female representatives has continually increased. Amplifying the voices of women in government is part of her vision. Since 1998, she has served five consecutive terms as a Member of Parliament in Mongolia.

In 2000, she founded Mongolia's Civil Will Party, which ran on a platform of good governance and clean politics. (This was practically unheard of in Mongolia at that time due to decades of corruption.) The Civil Will Party, which takes the concept of green liberalism as its ideology, believes that liberal democracy and the environmentalism of green politics must converge in order to build a sustainable future. Oyun Sanjaasuren founded the Zorig Foundation in honor of her brother. It is a prominent Mongolian NGO dedicated to advancing democracy and good governance in Mongolia. She also chairs Special Olympics Mongolia and has been actively advocating for the rights of children with disabilities. As if that wasn't enough, she was also the first president of the UN Environment Assembly, the governing body of United Nations Environment.

The World's Women Forum, held in Mongolia's capital, Ulaanbaatar, in August 2024, was a testament to her tireless work to increase female participation in politics. During the session on the topic "Towards Gender Equal Economies," Oyun Sanjaasuren emphasized Mongolia's current green transition as an opportunity for gender inclusivity and support for women-led energy-efficient small- and medium-sized enterprises.

Mina Susana Setra—Guardian of Indigenous Sovereignty

Mina Susana Setra is descended from the Dayak Pompakng people of West Kalimantan, Indonesia. Throughout the centuries, her people have developed an intricate and sacred relationship with the forest. It has not only been their home but provides food, medicines, and raw materials with which they make hunting weapons, build long houses, and carve wooden objects for storytelling.

Her parents were rubber tappers, and she fondly remembers going into the forest with them. She has described rowing in a canoe with her brother and a house filled with the sweet fragrance of tropical fruits such as rambutan and durian. Forests and rivers are part of the Dayak culture and identity, and cherished traditions have evolved in connection to their ancestral territory. Tragically, Setra's childhood home and forest were destroyed and converted into a palm oil plantation in 1976.

As a result of coercion, violence, and inadequate compensation for displacement, social problems like alcohol use, gambling, prostitution, and poverty have risen among the Dayak. The loss of her home and cultural identity has been the impetus for Mina Susana Setra to become one of the most passionate and effective activists to defend and protect the rights of indigenous peoples. In 1999, Mina became the Secretary General of the Indigenous Peoples' Alliance of the Archipelagos (AMAN), an Indonesian human rights and advocacy organization encompassing nearly 2,300 indigenous communities and approximately fifteen million people.

In 2012, Setra was instrumental in a review of the Forestry Law before the Constitutional Court, which made it illegal for the Indonesian government to claim the lands of indigenous groups and displace them. She is also president of If Not Us Then Who?, a global campaign to raise awareness of indigenous peoples' role in protecting our planet; the campaign educates through photography, filmmaking, creating content, and fostering exhibitions of local artwork.

Indonesia has the third-largest tropical forest area in the world. However, the country is one of the largest contributors to greenhouse gas emissions due to burning huge expanses of forest for palm oil and mining concessions. Protection of indigenous lands and sovereignty is both vital to Indonesia's well-being and critical to the rest of the world as our planet continues to heat up.

Cherrie Atilano—Champion for Female Farmers

While most twelve-year-old girls were hanging around with their friends and fussing about how to put on makeup or use a curling iron, Cherrie Atilano was out teaching sugar cane farmers how to grow their own food, compost food waste, and adopt more financially and environmentally sustainable practices.

Her father was a sugar planter, and young Cherrie loved to join in the work of planting and harvesting along with the workers. Unfortunately, her father died when she was still a child, so her family suffered financially. Her mother then had to care for Cherrie, her five siblings, and six adopted children all on her own. As a result, Cherrie's mom sent her to a scholarship center to learn practical skills such as cooking, sewing, and gardening.

Cherrie found a book on high-intensive gardening at the scholarship center's library. She learned, "When you're poor, 100 percent of your income goes to food, allocated 70 percent to rice and 30 percent [to other food items, a.k.a.] viand. However, when you know how to plant vegetables, you will save this 30 percent that may be used to send your children to school and have a roof over your head." This knowledge sparked a revelation in the precocious preteen, who realized that although there were many farmers where she lived, they all labored to grow and harvest sugarcane and did not grow their own food. Having learned about gardening and growing food at the scholarship center, she soon took steps to turn her knowledge into action.

For her twelfth birthday, Cherrie asked her mom for a bicycle; then she was able to visit sugar cane farmers in her free time. Cherrie taught them how to grow food in their backyard so they could save money and then use that savings to send their kids to school. This was a way to end the cycle of poverty that plagued many farmers who only grew sugar cane.

At fifteen, Cherrie was chosen for a scholarship to study agriculture at Visayas State University. She recalls those years as the most exciting time of her life as she juggled school, maintaining her scholarship, working part-time, sending money home to help her family, and taking on leadership positions at the university.

After graduation, Cherrie Atilano was quickly hired by a leading company to help them implement the best land practices with sustainable landscaping projects. Through her work, she always emphasized the need to respect farmers and compensate them fairly.

In 2014, Atilano was invited to the Vatican to meet Pope Francis, who advised her to "Capitalize on your passion." When she returned home, she founded Agrea, an innovative, agriculture-based business committed to empowering female farmers and promoting sustainability through food security and zero-waste initiatives.

Agrea has received many acknowledgements, including the United Nations's Global Compact Agriculture Business Excellence Award in 2017, the ASEAN Rural Poverty Eradication Leadership Award in 2019, and the COVID-19 Action Champion Award at the UN Women 2020 Asia-Pacific WEPs Awards.

As a child, Cherrie Atilano loved farming and had a clear vision of how she could improve it. She has grown up to become an agricultural activist and advocate, CEO of Agrea, and the UN's ambassador for nutrition.

"In the coming years, I am so excited to globally advocate for food and nutrition security as well as the promotion of regenerative agriculture."

—Cherrie Atilano

Maya Lin—an Architect Connecting the Past with the Future

Maya Lin weaves effortlessly between art, architecture, memory works, and environmental activism. In her book *Boundaries* she writes:

> I see myself existing between boundaries, a place where opposites meet: science and art, art and architecture, East and West. My work originates from a simple desire to make people aware of their surroundings.

Maya Lin was born in Athens, Ohio. Her father was a ceramicist and served as the dean of the College of Fine Arts at Ohio University, and her mother was a poet and English professor. Maya and her brother grew up in a household filled with art and intellectual curiosity, surrounded by the mossy hills and untamed woods of rural Ohio.

Lin was catapulted onto the national stage when she won the contest to reconceptualize the Vietnam Veterans Memorial. She was only nineteen and still finishing her architectural studies at Yale. Out of the nearly fifteen hundred anonymous entries in the competition, the eight jurors of the selection committee unanimously chose Maya Lin's design on May 6, 1981.

There was a storm of controversy over her minimalist and modern design, and because she was a young woman of Asian heritage. However, the committee strongly supported their choice, and the monument was finished and dedicated in 1982. Since then, its simple and elegant design, with a carved wall listing the names of over 58,000 men and women killed or missing in Vietnam, has served as a powerful memorial that touches the hearts of over five million people who visit each year.

After the Vietnam Veterans Memorial, she was commissioned to do more memory works, including the Civil Rights Memorial, the Yale Women's Table, and the Peace Chapel at a nature preserve near Juniata College. These varied projects clearly demonstrate Lin's ability to transform the major social and political issues of our time into three-dimensional art that inspires contemplation and healing. Lin's body of work, which includes buildings, large sculptures, public art, and earthworks, has become ever more wide-ranging and impressive in the decades since she won the contest.

She has always been concerned about environmental issues, and our current climate crisis has inspired her to establish *What is Missing?* (www.whatismissing.org), a multi-site memorial designed to raise awareness about the present sixth mass extinction of Earth's species—a human-caused event. Through a combination of artworks illustrating related scientific findings and an interactive online portal, Lin emphasizes that by protecting and restoring habitats, we can reduce carbon emissions and protect biodiversity. Lin considers this project to be her fifth and final memorial. She has also created a specific foundation for the cause, the What is Missing Foundation.

Maya Lin has received numerous awards, including the National Medal of Arts in 2009 and the Presidential Medal of Freedom in 2016. She is a member of the American Academy of Arts and Letters and the National Women's Hall of Fame. She was the subject of a film, *Maya Lin: A Strong Clear Vision* (1994), that won the 1994 Academy Award for Best Documentary, and an elementary school in California is named after her.

Nguy Thi Khanh—Fighting for Clean Air

Nguy Thi Khanh grew up in Bac Am, a rural village in northern Vietnam. Near her home, a coal-burning power plant spewed fumes and dust, causing terrible air pollution. She also witnessed many people in her community being diagnosed with cancer. As a result of being on the frontline of industrialized pollution, she has always been concerned about the air quality in Vietnam. She studied history, French, and diplomacy and planned to become a diplomat. However, her passion for the environment led her to work instead with a small Vietnamese nonprofit on water conservation issues and community development.

In 2011, Nguy Thi Khanh founded the Green Innovation and Development Center to promote sustainable energy, clean water and air protection, and green development. She learned everything she could about coal and climate change and worked with colleagues and officials to develop a different and more sustainable plan. She collaborated with energy experts and produced a 2013 study on the opportunity to reduce the coal share of the power supply mix in favor of sustainable energy sources.

The study detailed how expensive and risky coal was as a primary electric power source and proposed alternatives. After meticulous data collection and studies, Nguy Thi Khanh and her team proved that moving away from coal power plants and toward clean sources of energy production would benefit Vietnam financially and environmentally in the long run. In January 2016, the government announced its intention to review development plans for all new coal plants and affirmed Vietnam's commitment to responsibly implement shifts in energy production in accord with international commitments for reducing greenhouse gases. As a result of her efforts, Nguy Thi Khanh became the first Vietnamese to receive the distinguished Goldman Environmental Prize for her work in 2018.

It must be noted that despite the Vietnamese government's promises to move toward clean sources of energy, a sinister and corrupt vein has exposed itself in recent years. Several climate activists, including Nguy Thi Khanh, were arrested on trumped-up charges such as tax evasion. Fortunately, due to the concerted efforts of the international community and fellow Goldman Prize honorees to put pressure on the Vietnamese government, she was released from jail after being detained for sixteen months. As of February 2024, she is free, but as of this writing, a cleaner future for Vietnam is in peril.

Mana Saza—Leading Youths in Japan & Around the World to Fight Climate Change

In 2020, when the UN Climate Change Conference (abbreviated as COP26) was delayed due to the COVID-19 pandemic, Mana Saza decided that waiting was not an option. She saw that global warming wasn't slowing down, and the world needed to take action as soon as possible, so Saza worked with other young climate change experts from around the world to launch Mock COP, a platform through which young people and those in developing countries could make their voices heard.

A total of 330 young people from 140 countries attended the Mock COP. Online discussions centered around what policies the younger generation would establish if they participated in the actual COP26 conference. The Mock COP made it crystal clear that Generation Z is ready for the Anthropocene Age.

Saza served as the global coordinator for the mock conference. She organized the attendees' opinions into eighteen policy proposals and then presented them to various heads of state involved with the actual COP26.

The initiatives proposed by Saza and all those involved with MockCOP attracted worldwide attention and accolades, and they were invited to participate in the physical COP26 event, which was eventually held in 2021 in Glasgow, Scotland.

Mana Saza returned to Japan after graduating from University College London with a master's in sustainable development and founded SWiTCH, an educational space located in Shibuya, Tokyo. Through SWiTCH, she hosts workshops for students from elementary to high school and offers a free online toolkit called "Challenge 1.5°C" that allows people to understand climate change on a deeper level and implement methods for limiting planetary warming. The three pillars of SWiTCH's purpose are creating a resource circulation loop, encouraging climate-positive activities, and maintaining the richness of biodiversity.

Saza strongly feels that if young people and adults in Japan can see protecting the environment as a top priority and take immediate action, it will also raise Japan's international standing. When asked why she set up her office in Shibuya, Saza explained, "Shibuya is known to people around the world for its busy crossing. But think about the major impact it would have on the world if we could 'green' this town."

Forbes chose to include Mana Saza on its list of Japan's Thirty Under Thirty 2023 in the Business & Finance & Impact category.

"The climate crisis is an imminent threat, and we cannot postpone solving this issue. Therefore, we need to provide spaces for youths to actively participate in activities that will have a socio-environmental impact and where they can be trained to take ownership of climate-related issues."

—Mana Saza

Sasibai Kimis—Entrepreneur for Women and for the Earth

Sasibai Kimis was living the privileged life of an investment advisor in the UK when she experienced an unexpected wake-up call: due to spending long hours at work, she fell asleep while driving. Fortunately, she did not crash her car or injure anyone, but it was one of those pivotal moments when a message was being communicated from a higher source. In Kimis's case, she heard the message loud and clear.

She took time off and traveled to Hawaii to learn organic farming, and then in 2011, she also went to Cambodia, where she volunteered her time teaching English and helping to build schools. While she was in Kampong Thom, she visited a shelter and saw a little girl who was sitting by herself looking traumatized and crying. When she found out that the six-year-old girl had just been rescued from a brothel, Kimis decided that she had to drastically change her life and use her education and skills to help marginalized women and girls.

Sasibai Kimis had always wondered why it is that when there is so much wealth in the world, so much poverty exists, and why people go hungry even though so much food is produced. In an interview, she declared,

"People who have money don't care to do good, and people who are doing good never have enough money." This paradox became the catalyst for Kimis's venture.

At first, she had no intention of starting a business. But to support female artisans' work, she purchased handmade goods from women in rural communities, brought them home, and sold them to friends. After much thinking about how best to use her background in finance, she founded Earth Heir, a business that features handmade heirloom crafts from Malaysia. The goal is to support women and to create a sustainable monetary exchange in which women's work is valued for its quality and beauty. Kimis strongly believes that there is room within a capitalist paradigm to be fair and realize a decent profit—a way of doing business that is genuinely mutually beneficial.

Initially, she did everything herself, including pop-ups where she pitched a tent, opened a table, and peddled the goods from her inventory. Earth Heir was not profitable for the first three years, and Kimis was draining her savings. Luckily, just as she was about to give up, she received funding in the form of a British Consul Enterprise Award Grant, which gave her enough capital to renovate a space and invest in more inventory. Earth Heir is a certified B corporation whose mission is to preserve heritage artisanship, support refugee artisans, create sustainable livelihoods, and offer fair pricing.

Sasibai Kimis is now sharing what she has learned in the past decade by providing consulting and teaching others who want to learn from what her business Earth Heir has accomplished in accord with its motto: "To build nations and generations as heirs of the Earth."

Varshini Prakash—Shining a Light on Climate Change

Varshini Prakash experienced the disastrous power and potential of the elements firsthand when she was just eleven years old: her grandparents' home in Chennai, India, was damaged when a tsunami hit, causing severe flooding that reached their apartment in a high-rise building. This later inspired her to work to stem the tide of worldwide climate destabilization.

In college, she joined the fossil fuel divestment movement and played a significant role in getting the University of Massachusetts to sever its financial ties with big oil companies. Prakash is also the cofounder of an organization called the Sunrise Movement and was its executive director from 2010–2022. The Sunrise Movement is composed primarily of young people working to stop climate change and support the Green New Deal. Varshini was the voice of the Sunrise Movement and led a mass demonstration in solidarity with Rep. Alexandria Ocasio-Cortez that went viral.

Prakash's work has been featured on Democracy Now! and the BBC as well as in the *New Yorker*, *Teen Vogue*, the *Washington Post*, and more. She was recently named to the Grist Top Fifty Fixers for "people cooking up the boldest, most ambitious solutions to humanity's biggest challenges." She is also coeditor of the book *Winning the Green New Deal: Why We Must, How We Can*, and is a contributor to *The New Possible: Visions of Our World Beyond Crisis*.

Varshini Prakash appeared in the 2022 documentary film *To the End*, which focuses on the effects of climate change.

Tori Tsui—Giving Voice to Eco-Anxiety and Hope

In many ways, Tori Tsui is voicing what so many of us feel about the climate crisis but don't have the vocabulary to express—a sense of inner struggle and looming depression. In her debut book, *It's Not Just You*, Tsui sought out climate activists at the frontlines and asked them about their climate-related mental health struggles and then drew a connection between our collective despair and the systemic issues of racism, sexism, capitalism, and even ableism.

Tori Tsui was born in Hong Kong and is proudly Eurasian. She is a beautiful living tapestry of Cantonese, Taiwanese, Macanese, Vietnamese, English, Welsh, Finnish, and Turkish heritage. As a woman of Asian ancestry living in the UK, Tori understands that many don't value the voices of those who are not from a white, privileged background. As a result of her own experiences with racism, she advises Asian environmentalists to use their voices to communicate with clarity and purpose to dispel negative stereotypes of Asian women being docile and quiet.

Having studied ecology and conservation science, Tsui is now devoting 100 percent of her time to raising awareness about climate change and bringing communities together for global action as we struggle with a sixth mass species extinction. In addition to publishing her book, she has effectively disseminated her climate-centric message through collaborations with celebrities such as Stella McCartney, Billie Eilish, and Brian Eno highlighting the multifaceted problems of the Anthropocene Age. She has also spoken on global stages such as at the New York Times Climate Hub with Emma Watson and Malala Yousafzai and at the Southbank Center with Greta Thunberg.

She is a Senior Advisor for the Fossil Fuel Non-Proliferation Treaty and the Climate Justice Lead for EarthPercent (a climate foundation established by Brain Eno). She was featured in *Overheated*, a short film directed by Yassa Khan in which Billie Eilish, Maggie Baird (Eilish's mom), Tori Tsui, and other activists openly share their personal mental and emotional struggles with climate catastrophe amid ominous portents of a bleak future.

In 2019, Stella McCartney sponsored Tsui's participation in the Sail for Climate Action Project by sailing to COP25 (the UN Climate Change Conference) instead of jumping on a fuel-burning airplane.

In the last paragraph of *It's Not Just You*, Tori Tsui invites us to have hope even though we may feel paralyzed:

Radical imagination offers respite from this, allowing for the possibility of something better through carefully considered and collective means. To move away from It's Not Just You to It's Just Us and the Future We Create is an invitation to honor the power of community and shared understanding of where we are now and where we need to go.

Qiyun Woo—Helping the World Decipher the Science of Climate Crisis

Qiyun Woo started as an environmental activist at a young age and hasn't slowed down since. She holds a degree in environmental science from the National University of Singapore and works as a sustainability consultant.

In 2018, she started the Instagram account @theweirdandwild to help people navigate the complex issues of environmental degradation and the policies enacted to remedy these problems and save our planet. The Weird and Wild page was born from the idea that nature is not necessarily pretty and never tame, but it is wonderfully "wild" and sometimes "weird."

Woo feels it is an immense privilege to have her voice heard via the platform she has built and highlights the importance of keeping this space safe and inclusive so that everyone feels welcome and respected. In addition to The Weird and Wild page, she cohosts an environmental podcast on Southeast Asia called *Climate Cheesecake*. The podcast aims to break down complex climate topics into bite-size and easily digestible content.

In 2023, Woo was an official attendee at the COP28 climate conference in Dubai, where she used her social media savvy and gift for storytelling to show people around the world why it matters to care about climate issues from a Southeast Asian perspective. She is also a National Geographic Young Explorer and has been listed by the BBC on their list of 100 Inspiring Women of 2023.

"We need to confront the scary realities of a climate-impacted world and be ready to make the necessary trade-offs in order for us to thrive. Our current ways of working and living are fundamentally incompatible with a healthy planet."

—Qiyun Woo

CHAPTER NINE

AWESOME ACTIVISTS— FIGHTING FOR EQUALITY AND SOCIAL JUSTICE

When it comes to the good fight, the most courageous and determined fight their battles with powerful, nonviolent acts. In a world torn apart by endless strife and senseless wars, women are out there every day, fighting the good fight. From fierce activists to politicians to journalists, fearless females are tenaciously battling negative forces that endanger humanity while also creating a more beautiful and peaceful world that we all know is possible.

Anoyara Khatun—Saving Children, Changing the World

Anoyara Khatun comes from a family of little means in West Bengal. When she was just five years old, she also lost her father. When she turned twelve, her family's financial circumstances compelled her mother to listen to the advice of a distant relative, who suggested sending her to a family who could take care of her and give her an education. However, Anoyara and her mother had been deceived—she became a victim of child trafficking and was forced to work as a domestic servant in Delhi instead. There, she was abused, lived in terrible conditions, and was unable to contact her family until she was rescued by the organization Save the Children. When she returned home and saw how many children were suffering that same way, she became an avid children's rights activist. She has fought against exploitation and child marriage and has helped rescue hundreds of children. Her efforts led to her becoming one of the youngest recipients of the Nari Shakti Award.

"Children will have wings, won't be afraid of anything, and are able to reach to the skies."

—Anoyara Khatun

Raden Adjen Kartini—Warrior Wielding Words Against Forced Marriages

Raden Adjen Kartini, born in 1879, was a Javanese princess who gave up the chance to go to college abroad and acquiesced to a forced marriage to a man much older, becoming his fourth wife and stepmother to his seven children. Tragically, she died at just twenty-five years old, four days after giving birth to a son, yet she still escaped the walls that confined her with her words and became a pioneer for women's rights in Indonesia. Today, she is celebrated as a clear voice for gender equality. She can be considered the first to challenge Indonesian women's condition in society and the institution of marriage.

Kartini's story is one of irony and is a lamentable example of how even forward-thinking parents can succumb to ingrained patriarchal norms that significantly harm girls and women. Her father was the Regent of Jepara, located in central Java. He was a "liberated" man who allowed his daughters to learn how to read and write. He also had two wives, and since Kartini's mother was his second wife, Kartini was separated from her mother and raised by his primary wife.

Kartini was incredibly intelligent; even as a young girl, she was already thinking independently about how polygamy, colonialism, and capitalism exploited females in her country. As she grew older, she expressed her inward drive to activism by journaling and writing letters to her siblings and friends. One of those friends was Rosa Abendanon, wife to a Dutch educator stationed in Java. The two women became fast friends, and even after Rosa and her husband left Indonesia, Kartini sent Rosa long, wide-ranging missives that expressed her potent inner thoughts. She wrote that women in Indonesia were required to get married in order to be admitted to society as humans. Kartini rebelled against her fate by writing, "I long to be free, to be able to stand alone, to study, not to be subject to anyone, and, above all, never, never, to be obliged to marry. But, we must marry, must, must."

In 1911, seven years after Kartini's untimely death, Rosa and her husband decided to publish a selection of Kartini's letters under the title *Through Darkness into Light*. The book became a bestseller, and the

Abendanons invested that money in a foundation that honored Kartini's work by building more schools for indigenous girls—the Kartini schools. The book was translated into several languages and reprinted many times. It inspired scores of women worldwide, including Eleanor Roosevelt, who wrote the foreword to the 1960 edition of Kartini's book.

Although Kartini, who had herself entered into a forced marriage, seemed unlikely to be a heroine for female empowerment, her words were powerful! They were her superpower weapon, one with which she championed gender equality in Indonesia and beyond. Every year on April 21, Indonesians celebrate Kartini Day, and in 1963, she was declared a national hero by Sukarno, the first president of Indonesia.

Grace Lee Boggs—100 Years of Activism

"We are not subversives. We are struggling to change this country because we love it."

—Grace Lee Boggs

Grace Lee Boggs (born Grace Chin Lee) spent her entire life working for social justice and racial equality. She was born in 1915 in Rhode Island and died in 2015 in Detroit. Her parents were immigrants from China, and she and her siblings led a comfortable middle-class life. She entered Barnard College at sixteen and went on to earn a PhD in philosophy from Bryn Mawr College. She was especially drawn to the works of Marx, Hegel, and Margaret Mead.

Despite her stellar academic credentials, she wasn't able to get a decent job due to discrimination against "Orientals." Eventually, she got a position at a library in Chicago that paid only $10 per week. The only apartment she could afford was a tiny basement in a rat-infested ghetto neighborhood. Her experiences there opened her eyes to the plight of the marginalized.

One day, as she walked through her neighborhood, she encountered a group of people protesting poor living conditions, including the rat-infested housing. This encounter connected her with the Black community for the first time, and she realized that collective action was needed to effect changes for marginalized communities. In the 1950s, she moved to Detroit, where she edited *Correspondence*, a radical newspaper that was part of the movement for a worker-based revolution.

In 1953, Grace Lee met James Boggs, a charismatic and radical African American auto worker, activist, and intellectual from Alabama. She asked him to dinner, and that same evening, he proposed to her. Their marriage would last for forty years until James' death in 1993. They were partners in life, philosophy, and activism. They influenced and had meaningful dialogues with the most important human rights activists of the twentieth century, including Martin Luther King, Malcolm X, and Angela Davis. During the upheavals of the 1960s, she and her husband were among of the city's most noted activists, promoting issues that included environmentalism, feminism, Black power, and labor and civil rights. The FBI had a thick file on Grace Lee Boggs for the many rallies and protests that she attended.

She was a prolific writer and wrote many books, including *The Next American Revolution* and *Living for Change*, an autobiography. She turned her humble home in Detroit into a hub for discussions and creative solutions to the most pressing social issues of our time. In her later years, she created Detroit Summer, a program that connected hundreds of young volunteers to local neighborhoods where they planted community gardens and worked with schoolchildren. She also helped create the Boggs Center, an organization committed to helping activists develop into leaders and critical thinkers.

In 2012, there was a documentary made about Boggs by documentarian Grace Lee (not a relative or connected to Grace Lee Boggs), *American Revolutionary: The Evolution of Grace Lee Boggs*. Boggs remained active and involved with her many community-based initiatives until just before her death at 100.

Patsy Takemoto Mink—Blazing a Path for Equal Opportunity

Born in 1927 on the island of Maui, Patsy Takemoto Mink became a pioneer for women in politics as the first woman of color elected to the House of Representatives and the first Asian woman to serve in Congress. A lesser-known fact is that Mink was the first Asian American female candidate for the presidency of the United States. She was drawn into politics in response to the social prejudices of the day.

Her family had been in Hawaii for generations, and her father was a college-educated land surveyor working on sugar cane plantations in a managerial position. Patsy enjoyed a comfortable childhood growing up in Maui. She was valedictorian of her high school class and then attended the University of Hawaii.

In preparation for getting into medical school, Patsy Takemoto got degrees in zoology and chemistry, and she applied to many graduate schools in hopes of fulfilling her dream of becoming a doctor. However, she was turned down again and again due to her gender and her race. The lasting effect this had on her was to steel her determination to fight for gender and racial equality, as well as for marginalized people. She decided to study law instead; in 1947, she was accepted at the University of Nebraska, but she ended up leaving due to discrimination as the school would not allow her to live in the same dorm as white students. She ended up at the University of Chicago Law School, where she was one of two women and one of two Asian Americans to graduate. She also met John Mink, a geology student, who would in time become her husband and strongest supporter.

After graduation, she had difficulty getting a job in the legal profession because of the same sexism and racial discrimination that had dogged her early adulthood since college—now including prejudice against her interracial marriage with John Mink—so she started her own legal practice. Mink was the first Japanese American woman to practice law in her home state of Hawaii and worked as a private attorney for the House of Representatives in that territory.

Mink repeatedly challenged the status quo: as a congresswoman, she fought for gender and racial equality, affordable childcare, and bilingual education and became a major supporter of Title IX. She was one of the authors and sponsors of the Title IX law, which states, "No person in the United States shall, on the basis of sex, be excluded from participation in, be denied the benefits of, or be subjected to discrimination under any education program or activity receiving Federal financial assistance."

In 1972, she ran as an anti-war candidate in the 1972 Democratic presidential primary in Oregon. Although Mink lost, she was the first woman to vie for the US presidency! In 2014, she was posthumously awarded the Medal of Freedom by President Barack Obama. On March 25, 2024, the US Mint released the Patsy Takemoto Mink Quarter, the twelfth coin in the American Women Quarters Program. As a final salute to her indelible work on behalf of equal opportunity for women and girls, Title IX has also been renamed the Patsy Mink Equal Opportunity and Education Act.

Gwendolyn Mink

Gwendolyn Mink is Patsy and John Mink's only child. She was born in Chicago and has a PhD from Cornell University. Like her mother, Gwendolyn is an activist and has devoted her life to addressing inequalities for women and marginalized communities. She is the author of many books, including a biography of her mother entitled *Fierce and Fearless: Patsy Takemoto Mink, First Woman of Color in Congress,* which was coauthored with Judy Tzu-Chun Wu.

Gwendolyn Mink is a professor of politics at the University of California at Santa Cruz, where she educates and shapes the hearts and minds of future leaders.

Zin Mar Aung—Defender of Democracy

Myanmar (formerly known as Burma) was under British colonial rule from 1868–1948. Since its independence, the country has struggled in the grip of military rule, dictatorships, and civil wars for decades. With a population of fifty million people—one that is comprised of 130 minority groups speaking over 100 languages—it is also one of the poorest countries in Southeast Asia.

Zin Mar Aung was a young college activist protesting for freedom and democracy. She had a keen interest in political and social studies but had

to enroll in botany because the study of political science was forbidden
by the government. She hunted down as much information as she could,
taught herself about the principles of democracy, and protested in
the streets.

In 1998, at the age of twenty-two, she was arrested and sentenced to
twenty-eight years in jail without a trial. The length of her jail sentence
was seven years each for four offenses, one of which was for reading a
poem. She spent nine years in jail, most of it in solitary confinement, and
was often blindfolded and not allowed to wash or have access to books.
She did a lot of reflection and meditation to get through it and survive.

To her utter surprise and relief, Zin Mar Aung was suddenly released
before the start of her tenth year in jail. She stayed true to her cause; after
having been a prisoner of conscience, she jumped right back into taking
political action to push her country toward democracy. She started the
Yangon School of Political Science with friends and colleagues to train
political activists. Then, she cofounded the Rainfall Gender Studies
Group to promote women's participation in democracy. Their motto:
"We will think what others dare not think."

In 2012, US Secretary of State Hillary Clinton awarded Zin Mar Aung
the International Women of Courage Award. The World Economic
Forum nominated her for the World Global Leader award in 2014. That
same year, she was selected as a Reagan-Fascell Democracy Fellow of
the National Endowment for Democracy program. She was also invited
to the White House and met with Michelle Obama and Hillary Clinton.
As of 2024, Zin Mar Aung is the acting foreign minister of Myanmar;
however, as of this writing, the future of Myanmar is again in jeopardy
and civil war has broken out once more.

Lee Tai-young—Using the Law to Defend Women

Although Lee Tai-young's mother was not educated, she firmly believed in gender equality in education. As a result, her daughter went to school and graduated from Ewha Women's University with a degree in home economics and a desire to further her education and become a lawyer.

In 1936, Lee Tai-young married a Methodist minister, Chyung Yil-hyung, who had studied in the US. They had three daughters and a son. He was very forward-thinking and encouraged her to study law. However, she had to delay her studies due to the Japanese occupation of Korea in the early 1940s. Yil-hyung was accused of being a spy for the US and arrested and jailed on sedition charges. While her husband was in prison, Lee had to earn a living to support their children, so she worked as a school teacher and a radio singer and even took in sewing and washing.

After World War II, Lee entered Seoul National University, where she was the first woman ever to enroll. She earned her law degree at age thirty-eight while raising three children; she later earned her doctorate there as well. In 1957, she became the first woman in Korea to pass the National Judiciary Exam and the first female lawyer in the country's history. In the same year, she founded the Women's Legal Counseling Center, dedicated to helping poor women and their families.

Lee has authored fifteen groundbreaking books covering women's legal issues in South Korea, including her immensely popular 1972 book *Commonsense in Law for Women*. Lee and her all-female legal team also lobbied successfully for legislative changes to South Korean laws that disadvantaged women.

Her legacy lives on today. The Women's Counseling Center, which has been transformed into the Korea Legal Aid Center for Family Relations, still serves thousands of women every year.

"No society can or will prosper without the cooperation of women."

—Lee Tai-young

Jannatul Ferdous Ivy—Shero Standing Up for Burn Victims

Jannatul Ferdous, also known as Ivy to her friends, was on her way to a bright career. She was studying physics in an honors program in college when an accidental fire at home caused burns over 60 percent of her body. Her injuries were so severe that doctors feared she would not survive. While she was struggling for her life in the hospital, she overheard a distant relative say to her parent that they should poison her. "What's the point of being a woman and looking like that?" Those words were seared into Ivy's psyche. Fortunately, many people supported her with unconditional love, especially her grandparents, and she lived.

However, she has needed over fifty surgeries, including skin grafts and plastic surgery, to restore movement to her limbs. She still suffers considerably, especially from any irritation to her skin, as it is the largest organ. Even a 10 percent burn can permanently damage nerve endings.

Ivy returned to school but decided to pursue literature and developmental studies degrees instead of physics. She now has a master's degree in English and degrees in developmental studies and law. After her studies, Ivy joined Action on Disability and Development, which connected her to thousands of disabled persons across Bangladesh. However, there were no burn victims in the group, which made Ivy realize that a dedicated support system needed to be established.

As a burn survivor and a woman, Ivy has had to overcome a lot of discrimination and shaming from society. Now, she is helping other women and giving them the strength and resiliency to be part of society with dignity and respect. To further the cause, she is also the founder and executive director of Voice & Views, an NGO working on establishing the rights of burn survivors. Established in 2014, this small organization receives little funding, but as Ivy has said, every challenge makes her work even harder.

Voice & Views promotes the dignity, inclusion, and empowerment of women with disabilities in Bangladesh through awareness campaigns, capacity-building programs, policy advocacy, and networking with other stakeholders.

Jannatul Ferdous Ivy has also been using her talents as a storyteller, photographer, and filmmaker to bring consciousness to the needs of burn victims. She has written eleven books, and her feature film, *Article 16*, showcased workplace harassment of disabled women. In 2023, the BBC named her one of the top 100 women making a positive change in the world.

Mu Sochua—Exiled Twice, But Not Defeated

Mu Sochua was born in 1954 in Rangoon, Cambodia. By the time she reached her late teens, the Vietnam War was spilling into her country, and in 1972, her parents sent her and her sister to France to keep them safe. She never saw her parents again. After the Khmer Rouge took control, her parents perished along with millions of others in the terrible genocide that followed.

Mu Sochua eventually attended university in California and settled in the US. She married and had three daughters, one of whom is also an activist.

In 1989, after eighteen years in exile, she returned to a devastated country with her husband and their three daughters. She was determined to take part in the rebuilding of her beloved homeland and bring equality to women and improve rights for children, since Cambodia had one of the worst problems concerning trafficking of girls and women in the world.

In 1995, after a few years of campaigning, she won a parliament seat representing the Battambang district. Soon afterward, she was asked to lead the Ministry of Women and Veterans' Affairs. Ironically, she was the first woman to hold the position and became one of only two women in the cabinet.

As minister, Mu Sochua campaigned tirelessly to prevent violence against women and to end the exploitation of female workers. She helped draft a national law against domestic violence, negotiated an agreement with Thailand to curtail human trafficking in Southeast Asia, and launched a campaign to engage NGOs, law enforcement officials, and rural women in a national dialogue. Beyond protection measures, she knew that the only way to implement lasting changes was to get women into politics, so she traveled far and wide, visiting many remote villages and urging women in grassroots communities to run as local candidates. Due to her activism and leadership, 25,000 women ran for office in their local elections, and over 2,200 won. From 2013–2017, Mu Sochua was a member of the Cambodian parliament.

Unfortunately, the momentum toward gender equality and overall democracy was too threatening for the dictatorial rule of Hun Sen, and he proclaimed this movement a "rebellion." Prime Minister Hun Sen, who had been in power since 1985, shut down any semblance of democracy in Cambodia, and opposition leaders championing free elections and fundamental human rights were arrested and jailed, while many freedom fighters had to flee the country, including Mu Sochua. In 2017, she went into exile yet again. However, she continues the struggle for justice by rallying Cambodians overseas to take political action and organize opposition against Hun Sen and his corrupt government.

Today, Mu Sochua's work focuses on finding different avenues to rally resistance against Hun Sen, including through lobbying foreign political actors. The overarching goal is to find nonviolent means to reintroduce free and fair elections and allow freedom of speech and political dissent in Cambodia. She is also currently a board member of ASEAN Parliamentarians for Human Rights.

Mo Sochua's daughter, Devi Leiper O'Malley, inspired by her mother's activism, has established her own channels of feminist empowerment by becoming a leading feminist organizer working with nonprofits for social justice and targeted philanthropy.

In 2021, O'Malley cofounded Closer Than You Think, a hybrid ideas studio and consulting collective. She is now an independent consultant

working with feminist funds and serves on the board of the Urgent Action Fund for Women's Human Rights: Asia & Pacific.

Kanitha Wichiencharoen—Champion for Women from Home Life to Religious Life

Kanitha Wichiencharoen led a full life, from daughter to wife to mother to grandmother, and then became a nun. She was also a Thai lawyer and a women's rights advocate for many years. In all her roles, she consistently defended and advocated for the rights of girls and women. After her children were all grown, she became a *maechee* ("respected mother"), a Buddhist Theravadan nun. Noted for her human rights work with women, she established the first emergency shelter for women in Thailand and wrote legislation to protect women's rights. She also established the Association for the Promotion of the Status of Women.

As part of her work supporting women's health, Wichiencharoen developed a clinic dedicated to assisting and caring for pregnant women. With a one million baht donation from former US President Jimmy Carter and his wife, Rosalynn Carter, the Jimmy-Rosalynn Carter Women's Clinic and Nursery was established in 1987, providing care in the event of unplanned pregnancies and all other health needs of mothers as well as newborns. Through her work in building shelters and accommodating basic needs, Wichiencharoen helped tens of thousands of women and children who were victims of rape and abuse during her long life.

Even as she struggled with life-threatening cancer, she founded Mahapajapati Theri College, a place for women to gain a bachelor's degrees in Buddhism and philosophy in collaboration with the Thai Nuns Institute. Kanitha Wichiencharoen passed away in 2002 after a long battle with cancer, leaving a legacy of having made a real difference to the lives of so many of her sisters.

Tammy Duckworth—the Unstoppable

On April 19, 2018, Tammy Duckworth brought Maile, her six-day-old newborn daughter, to the US Senate floor with her. Senator Duckworth became the first US senator ever to cast a vote while holding a baby. Describing Duckworth as a trailblazer is an understatement because she has faced incredibly daunting challenges that would have defeated any mere macho man.

Ladda Tammy Duckworth was born in Thailand in 1968. Her mother is Thai, and her father is American. During her early childhood, the family moved to many different places in Asia, and young Tammy experienced racial taunts because she was a girl of mixed race, a.k.a. "Amerasian." The family eventually settled in Hawaii; while Tammy was in high school, their financial situation was so dire that they had to go on welfare. Tammy worked odd jobs, including vending bouquets of roses by the roadside. Despite the family's financial hardships, she stayed laser-focused on getting a college degree; she first attended the University of Hawaii and then earned a master's degree at George Washington University in 1992. She then moved to Chicago to pursue a PhD at Northern Illinois University but interrupted her education to serve in the military and only later completed her doctorate in 2015.

Duckworth had joined the US Reserve Officers' Training Corps (ROTC) in 1990 and was one of few women to train for combat missions; she even flew a Black Hawk helicopter. In 2004, she was deployed to Iraq with the Illinois Army National Guard when her helicopter was hit by an RPG missile, which landed on her lap and exploded. Miraculously, the helicopter landed safely, but Tammy was severely injured, including losing both her legs.

While recovering in the hospital, a serendipitous opportunity presented itself when US Senator Dick Durbin of Illinois was seeking a wounded veteran to attend the State of the Union address—Duckworth happily volunteered. After the event, Durbin told her to contact him if she needed anything—and she did so again and again, not for herself, but on behalf of other veterans who needed help with problems like missing pension payments. Senator Durbin was impressed by her tenacity and deep concern for others even while she was struggling with her own situation.

A few months later, when Illinois's longtime congressman Henry Hyde announced he was retiring, Durbin asked her to consider running for the House of Representatives, and she took up the challenge. She lost that race by a 2 percent margin. But she did not give up!

After she was fully healed from the acute phase of her injuries, she became director of the Illinois Department of Veterans Affairs, where she helped create a tax credit for employers that hire veterans, established a first-in-the-nation 24/7 veterans crisis hotline, and developed innovative programs to improve veterans' access to housing and health care. Then she ran for Congress again, and this time she won! In 2012, Duckworth was elected to the US House of Representatives, and then reelected; and in 2016, she was elected to the US Senate.

Duckworth is the first Thai American woman to serve in Congress. She is also the first woman with a disability to have been elected to Congress, as well as the first female double amputee in the US Senate and the first US senator to give birth while in office. Then, in 2018, Senator Duckworth made headlines across America by being the first senator to bring a baby with her onto the Senate floor as she cast her vote. She (and her baby) changed Senate rules, allowing all Senators to bring their infants with them during votes as needed while their babies are under the age of one.

In her personal life, she and her husband have struggled with infertility. After many rounds of in-vitro fertilization (IVF), they had their first daughter, Abigail, in 2016, and two years later, their second daughter, Maile.

Senator Tammy Duckworth is a powerful advocate for gender equality, veterans' rights, and gun control. Her latest battle is to defend women's right to make decisions about their own bodies, including the right to IVF.

Malala Yousafzai—a Valiant Force for Good in the World

Malala Yousafzai is a Pakistani activist for female education and the rights of girls, as well as the youngest person ever to receive the Nobel Peace Prize. She was born in Mingora, Pakistan, in the country's Swat Valley in 1997. Her father, Ziauddin Yousafzai, believed that she would one day become a politician, and he often let her stay up late at night to discuss politics. She spoke about education rights for the first time at age eleven, when her father took her to the local press club in Peshawar, giving her perspective on the topic, "How dare the Taliban take away my basic right to education?" At this time, the Taliban was frequently blowing up girls' schools. When she heard that BBC Urdu news was looking for a schoolgirl to anonymously blog about her life—due to the fact that the girl who had been about to do it had changed her mind due to her family's fear of Taliban reprisals—Malala, who was only in seventh grade at the time, took on the task. BBC staff insisted she use a pseudonym: She was called *Gul Makai*, meaning "cornflower" in Urdu.

She wrote notes by hand, which were then passed to a reporter to be scanned and sent to BBC Urdu by email; her first post went up on January 3, 2009. Her descriptions continued to be published as military operations began, including the First Battle of Swat; eventually Malala's school was shut down. By January 15, the Taliban had issued an edict that no girls were allowed to go to school—and by this point, they had already destroyed over one hundred girls' schools. After the ban went into effect, they continued to destroy more schools. A few weeks later, girls were allowed to attend school, but only at coed schools; girls' schools were still banned, and very few girls went back to school in the atmosphere of impending violence that hung over the area. On February 18, local Taliban leader Maulana Fazlulla announced he would lift the ban on education of females; girls would be able to attend school until March 17, when exams were scheduled, but they would have to wear burqas.

After Malala finished her series of blog posts for the BBC on March 12, 2009, a *New York Times* reporter asked her and her father if she could appear in a documentary, and they went ahead with it. At this point, military actions and regional unrest forced the evacuation of the city of Mingora, and Malala was sent to stay with relatives in the countryside. In late July, her family was reunited and she was allowed to return home. After the documentary, Malala began to do some major media interviews. By the end of 2009, her identity as the BBC blogger had been revealed by journalists. She started receiving international recognition and was awarded a National Youth Peace Prize by her country's government, the first time Pakistan had awarded this prize. As things developed, she began to plan the Malala Education Foundation in 2012, whose purpose would be to help economically disadvantaged girls to be able to attend school. But in the summer of the year she was fifteen years old, a group of Taliban leaders agreed to kill her—in a unanimous vote. As she rode the bus home one day in October, 2012, a masked gunman shot her; the bullet passed through her head, neck, and shoulder, and then wounded two other girls.

Malala barely survived, but she was airlifted to a Peshawar hospital where doctors removed the bullet from her head in five hours of surgery. She then received specialized treatment in Europe, with the Pakistani government bearing the cost. Since her recovery, she has continued to speak out both for education for girls and for the rights of women in general. At age seventeen, she was the corecipient of the 2014 Nobel Peace Prize for her work on behalf of children and young people, sharing the prize with Kailash Satyarthi, an activist for the rights of trafficked children from India. Malala is the youngest Nobel laureate ever. That year, she also received an honorary doctorate from University of King's College in Halifax, Nova Scotia, Canada. On her eighteenth birthday, she opened a school in Lebanon not far from the Syrian border for Syrian refugees, specifically teenage girls, funded by the nonprofit Malala Fund. In 2020, Malala graduated from Oxford University with a degree in philosophy, politics, and economics. Learn more about her work at www.malala.org.

Yuri Kochiyama—a Patriot Who Practiced Radical Activism

Yuri Kochiyama (born Mary Yuriko Nakahara in 1921) enjoyed a happy childhood in San Pedro, California. Her father was a well-to-do fish merchant whose father had been a samurai, and her mother was a piano teacher. They lived in an affluent white neighborhood and were active in the local Presbyterian church. Yuriko graduated from Compton

College with a degree in English and journalism. But their comfortable middle-class life changed overnight with the bombing of Pearl Harbor on December 7, 1941.

Because Yuriko's father was known to be friends with the Japanese ambassador and had other prominent business contacts from Japan, he was tagged as a possible threat to US national security. The FBI descended on their home and arrested her father, Seiichi Nakahara, who had just returned home from surgery and was in poor health. After being detained for six weeks, Yuriko's father passed away one day after he was released. But before they even had a chance to mourn, the rest of the family, including her mother, Mrs. Tsuyako Nakahara, Yuriko's twin brother, Peter, and their older brother, Arthur, were "evacuated," eventually ending up at the War Relocation Authority internment camp in Arkansas. This life-shattering experience marked the beginning of Yuriko's political awakening and shaped her revolutionary spirit as she came to understand the harsh realities of racial prejudice.

During the family's two years under internment, Yuriko Nakahara met her future husband, Bill Kochiyama. He was in the US Army's 442nd Regimental Combat Team and had come to the camp in Arkansas on an official visit. It was love at first sight. While Bill was fighting on the front, she wrote letters to him every day, and soon after World War II ended, they married. In 1948, they moved to New York City and went on to have six children. Later, in the 1960s, they moved to Harlem and joined the Congress of Racial Equality, an African American civil rights committee.

Yuri and her husband both felt deep concern for social justice and human rights, and that shared passion was a defining aspect of their marriage. Although Bill did not always agree with Yuriko's more radical views, he always stood by her. In the 1980s, they worked together with other Japanese Americans to help bring about compensation for Japanese Americans who had been detained during World War II. In 1988, President Ronald Reagan signed the Civil Liberties Act, which authorized reparations to Japanese American World War II detainees. The couple also believed in Black rights; they became friends with Malcolm X and supported his work. Yuri Kochiyama was in the audience the day Malcolm X was assassinated. She immediately rushed toward him when he was shot and held his hand as he passed away.

Her commitment to social justice had no boundaries. She joined Puerto Rican Americans at their occupation of the Statue of Liberty, a protest that was part of the Puerto Rican fight for freedom from US colonialism. She supported political prisoners and victims of FBI oppression, taught English to immigrants, and volunteered in soup kitchens and homeless shelters in New York City. Kochiyama is widely respected for her work in forging unity among diverse communities, especially between Asian Americans and African Americans. She also built alliances with indigenous leaders, challenged Islamophobia, and spoke out in support of Korean comfort women and Japanese nuclear bomb survivors.

After her husband Bill died in 1993, Yuri continued the activism they had started together until her death in 2014 at the age of ninety-three. Yuri Kochiyama penned a memoir entitled *Passing It On* (2004), and Diane Fujino has written an excellent biography of her, *Heartbeat of Struggle: The Revolutionary Life of Yuri Kochiyama*.

Tashi Zangmo—Advocate for Buddhist Nuns in Bhutan

Tashi Zangmo is from a family of nine children and was the first girl in her village to attend school. She was born in 1963 in Wamrong, one of the most remote villages in the far-flung Kingdom of Bhutan.

Her school was very distant from her village, so as a child, Tashi had to live there through sixth grade in order to go to school. Since all the other students at the time were boys, she had to sleep by herself in the corner of a cold room without even a mattress. But she endured the hardship because she wanted knowledge.

Zangmo tirelessly furthered her education, obtaining a degree in Buddhist philosophy from the Central Institute of Higher Tibetan Studies and a degree in developmental studies from Holyoke College in Massachusetts. She also went on to earn a master's degree and doctorate from the University of Massachusetts.

Although Bhutan is world-famous for its official Gross National Happiness policy, one which figured into her PhD thesis, there are still disparities, particularly in terms of gender-based inequality and violence. So when Tashi Zangmo completed her doctorate, she returned to her home country, where she has worked diligently ever since on behalf of both girls and women in secular life and nuns.

Zangmo believes there must be a balance between material and spiritual needs. Therefore, she clearly understands that as Bhutan is pulled into the modernized world of technology and commerce, supporting women in monastic life is critical to preserving the country's ancient culture and its rich Buddhist traditions.

The Bhutanese government provides funds for male monks and their monasteries, but there was no support for nunneries, with the result that many nuns had to contend with poor living conditions and hardship to follow their spiritual path. So Tashi Zangmo laid the groundwork for the Bhutan Nun Foundation, which raises funds to build better nunneries and provide higher education for the nuns, allowing them to better serve their communities as teachers and community leaders. She has been the foundation's executive director since 2009. The Queen Mother of Bhutan, Her Majesty Gyalyum Sangay Choden Wangchuck, is an official sponsor and a great admirer of Zangmo's work.

Journalists

In a world where truth is becoming a casualty, journalists and reporters are one of the most precious assets we have to help us navigate the precarious junction between what is true as opposed to trumped-up lies and propaganda. These five sheroes of truth-telling are shining role models for everyone searching for substance and real news.

Connie Chung—First Asian Female News Anchor & Next Generation Inspiration

"Good reporters are genuinely curious and interested in hearing people's stories, and that helps you gain trust. I would go grocery shopping, and people would start telling me their stories!"

—Connie Chung

In 1993, after several years of tenaciously working as a correspondent and a coanchor for NBC and CBS, Connie Chung was promoted to the same position at the prestigious *CBS Evening News*. She became the second woman (after Barbara Walters) to coanchor a major evening daily news broadcast. Her on-screen presence sparked a new era for women and Asians in TV journalism. Chung has also worked in other prime spots on NBC, CBS, ABC, and CNN, as well as cohosting a program on MSNBC with her husband, Maury Povich.

Connie Chung is the youngest of five sisters, and the only sibling to have been born in the US after her parents immigrated from China in 1945. The Chungs raised their girls to be very confident, but her older sisters overshadowed young Connie. Once her sisters left home, Connie found her voice: she participated in student government, followed politics, was an avid watcher of legendary news anchor Walter Cronkite, and copiously read news publications.

As a TV journalist, she was known for being a straight-arrow and a tough interviewer. When Connie Chung asked tough questions, quite a number of famous and notorious people she interviewed walked out of the room, including Bill Gates and controversial skater Tonya Harding.

Over the years, Chung has received many awards, but none of those accolades have moved her to tears like learning about "Generation Connie." The term is from the title of an article written by Connie Wang in which she explored why hundreds of women in their thirties and forties are named Connie. Well, as it turns out, they were named after Connie Chung! Asian American mothers wanted their daughters to grow up just like Chung, who is a model of professionalism, beauty, and brains.

Connie not only inspired Generation Connie, but has spurred on many other Asians, both female and male, to take chances and use their voice for the greater good, including Lisa Ling, another remarkable Asian shero of journalism.

Lisa Ling—Bravely Bringing Real News from Far Afield

In 1989, when Lisa Ling was just sixteen, she beat out scores of other hopefuls when she was chosen for a prime spot as a host of Scratch, a teen magazine TV show produced in Northern California.

There were only a few Asian Americans in her school; she was teased and felt bad that she looked different from her classmates. Despite that, she excelled academically and became a formidable debater and communicator. It was her debate coach who encouraged her to try out for the Scratch hosting spot, proving the effect one supportive adult can have on a student. Lisa Ling has since become one of the most remarkable and provocative investigative journalists of our time.

From her debut on the teen magazine show, she was spotted by a producer in New York who called and asked her to audition for a slot on a new educational television experiment called Channel One, a satellite news service broadcast directly into thousands of American schools. Ling won the job at age eighteen, thereby becoming the youngest reporter for the platform. She worked there for seven years and was seen by millions of students in over 12,000 schools nationwide.

She wasn't afraid to tackle challenging foreign assignments that required her to travel to places like Colombia, where she and her crew once filmed a cocaine bust, and Afghanistan at the height of its dangerous civil war, where she had to disguise herself as a Muslim woman to cover the story.

While Lisa Ling was honing her craft as an investigative reporter and becoming increasingly famous on TV, her mother and father were not happy with her pursuit since they were traditional Chinese parents who wanted her to become either a doctor or lawyer. Happily, she stayed with her career, and in 1999, she received an offer from Barbara Walters to join her top-rated daytime talk show, *The View*. Ling quickly became a favorite on the show, and ratings shot up by 15 percent. Although her plum role on *The View* significantly advanced Ling's career and gave her great exposure, she missed the exhilarating energy of reporting on hard news from the frontlines and traveling to remote locales to search for the real truth behind a story. In 2002, she left *The View* to join in creating the 2003 news series *National Geographic Ultimate Explorer*.

In her new job, Ling became the Indiana Jones of reporting: she embraced adrenalin-inducing assignments such as jumping out of an airplane for an adventure feature and trekking across the Himalayas to report on the illegal trade in the hide of the chiru, a rare and endangered Tibetan antelope. She entered the war zone in Baghdad during the US-Iraqi War and did an investigative story on incarcerated women in US and Indian prisons.

True to her passion for chasing unique stories, she has done fantastic reporting in collaboration with the Oprah Winfrey Network over the past two decades. Between 2014 and 2022, she hosted *This is Life with Lisa Ling*, a CNN docuseries. Her latest is *Take Out*, a docuseries about Asian American cuisine providing rich context and discussion around immigration, identity, and community.

In addition to all of her professional accomplishments, Lisa Ling has also found time for her family. She is married to Paul Song, a radiation oncologist, and they have two daughters. Connie Chung was an honored guest at their 2007 wedding.

Maria Ressa—Standing Up Against Dictators

Maria Ressa, who moved to New Jersey from the Philippines at age ten, later said of the experience, "I had to figure out what a short brown kid was going to do in this big white world." She figured it out by becoming one of the most respected journalists in the world.

Ressa attended Princeton University, where she studied English and theater, graduating *cum laude*. She also received a Fulbright Fellowship to study political theater at the University of the Philippines. After returning to her home country, Ressa immersed herself in investigative journalism and worked for CNN in several capacities, including as the bureau chief for Asia. She also cofounded *Rappler*, a digital news source that takes pride in providing uncompromising journalism. In 2019 and 2020, she was subjected to politically-motivated persecution widely seen as having been orchestrated by then Philippine president Rodrigo Duterte, but even an unjust arrest and prosecution couldn't stop her.

Ressa has been named one of *Time*'s Most Influential Women of the Century and has also been recognized by *Time* for her work against disinformation. She is an inaugural Carnegie Distinguished Fellow at Columbia University's newly launched Institute of Global Politics. In July 2024, Ressa will join Columbia University's School of International and Public Affairs as a professor of professional practice.

THE BOOK OF AWESOME ASIAN WOMEN

Alex Wagner—the Present and Future Face of Journalism

Alexander Swe Wagner was born in 1977 in Washington, DC. Her mother, who is from Burma (now known as Myanmar), immigrated to the US and became a naturalized citizen, and then attended Swarthmore College. Alex Wagner's father was born in Iowa and is of European descent. He was a prominent political strategist for Bill Clinton's presidential campaign in 1992.

Growing up, she identified as white and never really thought deeply about her Asian ancestry until someone asked her if she was adopted. Being asked this question caused Alex to delve into the ancestral heritage of both her parents, and it inspired her to write *Futureface: A Family Mystery, an Epic Quest, and the Secret to Belonging*, a personal memoir of her epic journey in search of the real story of her East-West heritage.

It is curiosity and thirst for truth that makes Alex Wagner one of the best political journalists today. In 2022, she became the first Asian American woman to anchor a primetime cable news show when she stepped in four days a week to fill Rachel Maddow's show slot on MSNBC. Wagner was a natural replacement for the highly popular Maddow because she has been tenacious in reporting in the US and abroad and has gathered a wealth of experience, including serving as both cohost and executive producer of Showtime's Emmy-nominated political docuseries *The Circus*. She also served as a special correspondent for CBS News and cohost of *CBS This Morning: Saturday*. She was previously also a senior editor at *The Atlantic* and a White House correspondent for *AOL's Politics Daily*.

Her show on MSNBC is *Tonight with Alex Wagner*, which airs in primetime hours Tuesday through Friday.

Alex Wagner is married to Sam Kass, who founded a food technology company after having been a personal chef for the Obama family and working with Michelle Obama's Food Initiative. Alex and Sam have two sons, Cy and Rafael.

Katie Phang—from the Courtroom to Her Own Show on MSNBC

Katie Phang wanted to be a pediatric immunologist when she was a kid—a rather specific goal for a youngster, but one that shows her natural propensity for details, a trait that is a hallmark of a good lawyer.

Although Phang did initially attend medical school in accord with her childhood dream, she switched to studying law. She found her stride as a prosecutor fresh out of college, working for the state attorney's office in Miami-Dade County. Her presence in the courtroom got the attention of local network WFOR-TV, and they asked her to join them as a legal consultant to help decipher the legal jargon and issues for audiences. In 2005, Phang covered the trial of Michael Jackson and other notable trials for WFOR. However, she did lose her position at the state attorney's office due to the incompatible status of being a consultant for a media platform while working as an assistant prosecutor. Undaunted, she quit her civil service job, continued as a media legal consultant, and went to work for a private law firm. She eventually started a litigation law practice in partnership with her husband, Jonathan Feldman. She also became a legal analyst for Fox News, appearing frequently on Greta Van Susteren's show, and then was hired as an analyst by NBCUniversal in 2017.

In 2022, MSNBC came calling and invited her to host her own show. After a lengthy discussion with her husband and young daughter, she jumped on board and launched *The Katie Phang Show*, where she helps her audience understand intersecting aspects of law, politics, and culture. In taking this opportunity, Phang also made history as one of the first Asian American women to host a top-tier cable news show under her own name. Her show airs every Saturday on MSNBC.

When asked how she got to where she is today, she has said the source of her work ethic was her Korean immigrant parents. Her father, who arrived in this country with next to nothing from South Korea, became a doctor and college professor. Her mother, also from South Korea, showered young Katie with tough love and demanded straight As. Despite her mom's disciplinary ways, on the occasion of her mom's birthday, Katie Phang declared, "A mother is your first friend, your best friend, your forever friend."

In 2023, Katie Phang hosted "The Culture Is: AAPI Women" as part of MSNBC's "The Culture Is" series. The special featured her talking with seven AAPI (Asian American and Pacific Islander) women who candidly discussed topics ranging from Asian American stereotypes to family honor and shame.

Who Are Your Awesome Asian Women?

Dear Reader,

There are so many more awesome Asian women who should be acknowledged and celebrated for their brilliance and contributions to the world, and we wish we could include them all in this book! Do you know of an awesome Asian woman, past or present, that we can include in a future volume?

Below is a simple nomination form.

Nominate Your Awesome Asian Woman

Bibliography

Please scan this QR code for the full bibliography and a bonus PDF of five more awesome Asian women.

The Book of Awesome Asian Women - Bibliography

About the Author

Karen Wang Diggs describes herself as a "history hound." Since she was a child, she has found uncovering the truth hidden between the pages of history books an irresistible pursuit. Behind every date and every significant event in history, there is a catalog of untold stories, and she's always been passionate about digging them up and understanding the people behind the events. Themes of social justice, gender equality, and racial equality infuse every aspect of her work.

As a woman, Diggs is passionate about discovering and sharing illuminating accounts of the injustices faced by women throughout history. She wants to empower women and girls to change the future and strive for absolute parity between the sexes. Her work is dedicated to sharing lesser-told stories to show the world that strong women have always been, and always will be, crucial to the future of the world.

Karen was born in Hong Kong but grew up in Hawaii. She was raised by a single mother whose strength and resilience fed into her passion for uncovering the life stories of strong women throughout history. After studying at the University of Hawaii, she moved to the rolling hills of San Francisco, where she became both a classically-trained chef and certified nutritionist. Living at the edge of the oldest Chinatown in America has added to her fascination with hidden stories of the Asian diaspora. When she's not writing or indulging in her book addiction, Karen Wang Diggs continues to cook up a storm as a professional chef while also deepening her understanding of history by pursuing a master's in anthropology.

Check out Karen's blog at:
www.herstoryinhistory.com

Follow Karen on Instagram:
@herstoryinhx

Contact Karen at:
storyteller@herstoryinhistory.com

Karen Wang Diggs is also a professional chef—
if you like, check out her food links!

Cooking blog:
www.kareniscooking.com

Instagram:
@kareniscooking

P.S.

Keeping Their Voices Alive

"I raise up my voice—not so that I can shout, but so that those without a voice can be heard... We cannot all succeed when half of us are held back."

—Malala Yousafzai

We've now met many incredible women, and I'm sure you'll agree that their stories deserve to be told. As much of the world still battles for gender equality, it's vital we remember that strong and courageous women have always existed—often in the face of significant difficulty.

It's my goal for the remarkable stories of these women to reach as many people as possible, serving as a reminder for every person who identifies as female that great and powerful women have always existed...and always will. These inspirational stories show us that no matter what, women are every bit as capable as men—no matter what societal programming wants us to believe.

Now I'd like to ask for your help in spreading these stories far and wide, allowing inspiration to reach even more people. Don't worry—it'll only take a few minutes.

By leaving a review of this book on Amazon, you'll show new readers where they can find these under-told stories—and make sure more people hear about these incredible women.

Simply by letting other readers know about your experience with this book and telling them what they can expect to find inside, you'll be shining a beacon of light and inspiration.

Thank you so much for your help. Let's work together to amplify the voices of awesome Asian women!

Amazon Book Review

Mango Publishing, established in 2014, publishes an eclectic list of books by diverse authors—both new and established voices—on topics ranging from business, personal growth, women's empowerment, LGBTQ studies, health, and spirituality to history, popular culture, time management, decluttering, lifestyle, mental wellness, aging, and sustainable living. We were named 2019 *and* 2020's #1 fastest growing independent publisher by *Publishers Weekly*. Our success is driven by our main goal, which is to publish high-quality books that will entertain readers as well as make a positive difference in their lives.

Our readers are our most important resource; we value your input, suggestions, and ideas. We'd love to hear from you—after all, we are publishing books for you!

Please stay in touch with us and follow us at:

Facebook: Mango Publishing
Twitter: @MangoPublishing
Instagram: @MangoPublishing
LinkedIn: Mango Publishing
Pinterest: Mango Publishing
Newsletter: mangopublishinggroup.com/newsletter

Join us on Mango's journey to reinvent publishing, one book at a time.